Flip

YOUR Classroom

Reach Every Student in Every Class Every Day

Jonathan Bergmann
Aaron Sams

iste

EUGENE, OREGON • WASHINGTON, DC

ASCD

ALEXANDRIA, VIRGINIA

Flip YOUR Classroom

Reach Every Student in Every Class Every Day

Jonathan Bergmann and Aaron Sams

Director of Book Publishing: *Courtney Burkholder*
Acquisitions Editor: *Jeff V. Bolkan*
Production Editors: *Lynda Gansel, Tina Wells*
Production Coordinator: *Emily Reed*
Graphic Designer: *Signe Landin*
Copy Editor: *Kristin Landon*
Proofreader: *Ann Skaugset*
Cover Design, Book Design, and Production: *Kim McGovern*

Library of Congress Cataloging-in-Publication Data

Bergmann, Jonathan.

Flip your classroom : reach every student in every class every day / Jonathan Bergmann and Aaron Sams.

p. cm.

ISBN 978-1-56484-315-9 (pbk.)

1. Video tapes in education. 2. Individualized instruction. 3. Teachers—Time management. 4. Homework. I. Sams, Aaron. II. Title.

LB1044.75.B47 2012

371.33'52—dc23

2011052647

First Edition

ISBN: 978-1-56484-315-9

Printed in the United States of America

Cover art: © Dreamstime.com/Tiplyashina

ISTE® is a registered trademark of the International Society for Technology in Education.

ASCD® is a registered trademark of the Association for Supervision and Curriculum Development. ASCD® product #112060

SUSTAINABLE FORESTRY INITIATIVE
Certified Sourcing
www.sfiprogram.org
SFI-00341
Label applies to the text stock

About ISTE

The International Society for Technology in Education (ISTE) is the trusted source for professional development, knowledge generation, advocacy, and leadership for innovation. ISTE is the premier membership association for educators and education leaders engaged in improving teaching and learning by advancing the effective use of technology in PK–12 and teacher education.

Home to ISTE's annual conference and exposition, the ISTE leadership conference, and the widely adopted NETS, ISTE represents more than 100,000 professionals worldwide. We support our members with information, networking opportunities, and guidance as they face the challenge of transforming education. To find out more about these and other ISTE initiatives, visit our website at www.iste.org.

To learn more, go to www.iste.org or call (toll-free in the United States and Canada) 1.800.336.5191.

About ASCD

Founded in 1943, ASCD (formerly the Association for Supervision and Curriculum Development) is an educational leadership organization dedicated to advancing best practices and policies for the success of each learner. Our 150,000 members in more than 145 countries are professional educators from all levels and subject areas—superintendents, supervisors, principals, teachers, professors of education, and school board members.

Our nonprofit, nonpartisan membership association provides expert and innovative solutions in professional development, capacity building, and educational leadership essential to the way educators learn, teach, and lead.

To learn more, go to www.ascd.org/learnmore or call (toll-free in the United States and Canada) 1.800.933.ASCD (2723) or 1.703.578.0600.

About the Authors

Jonathan Bergmann believes educators should ask one guiding question: What is best for my students in my classroom? To the best of his abilities he has done this in his 25 years as a high school science teacher. He received the Presidential Award for Excellence for Math and Science Teaching in 2002 and was named semifinalist for the Colorado Teacher of the Year in 2010. He is currently the lead technology facilitator for the Joseph Sears School in Kenilworth, Illinois. He is the father of three teenagers and is happily married to the love of his life.

Aaron Sams has been an educator since 2000. He received the Presidential Award for Excellence in Math and Science Teaching in 2009 and cochaired the committee to revise the Colorado Science Academic Standards. He regularly turns off all his electronic devices to spend time with his wife and three children, and he highly recommends implementing "unplugged Sundays" for those who struggle to power down and spend time with the ones who matter most. Aaron holds a bachelor of science degree in biochemistry and a master of arts in education, both from Biola University, Colorado. He is currently a classroom science teacher in Woodland Park, Colorado.

Acknowledgment

Thanks to The Morgridge Family Foundation and Techsmith Corporation.

Dedication

For Kris and Kelsey

Contents

Foreword

One cool, crisp, typically gorgeous Colorado morning in the fall of 2010, I found myself driving into Woodland Park at the base of Pikes Peak. I was on my way to observe two teachers at Woodland Park High School whom I already "knew" online but hadn't ever had a chance to meet in person.

I first "met" Jon Bergmann and Aaron Sams online sometime in 2007. I don't recall exactly when and in what context anymore, but I began to read about the "flipped" approach they were using in their chemistry classes. As a former math teacher and current director of technology for my high school, this fit in nicely with my ongoing efforts to try to figure out how to best use technology to meet the needs of our teachers and students.

I began to read (and watch) more about this model and conversed with Jon and Aaron in various online settings trying to learn more about the advantages—and disadvantages—of this approach. Right from the start, it was clear that they didn't think they had all the answers. They were very upfront about what was working, and what wasn't working; about which aspects of their approach they thought were rock solid, and which aspects were weak (and they were constantly asking questions to try to improve these). In an age of "silver bullets" in education, this was refreshing.

Eventually Brian Hatak, one of the chemistry teachers at my high school, decided to try to implement a flipped classroom approach, and we began to try to figure out together—with lots of help from Jon and Aaron from afar—how best to do this. (Oh, how I wish we'd had this book then.) Much like Jon and Aaron's experience, we learned tremendously from both our successes and our challenges.

When in the fall of 2010 I returned to the classroom to pick up one section of algebra in addition to my tech director duties (a result of budget cuts), I knew I wanted to try to learn from their experiences to try to implement my own version of a flipped classroom approach. I asked if I could come down and visit their classrooms.

Although no book is as good as visiting their classrooms, not everyone lives close enough to just drive down and visit. This book is the next best thing. It provides a window into a flipped classroom led by two educators who were driven by a simple question: "What is best for the students in my classroom?" Although they felt pretty good about their "traditional" teaching, they knew they could do better. The flipped classroom approach, like all good educational ideas, stemmed from the needs of their students. This book chronicles their journey from their first shaky steps at trying to "flip" their classrooms to their current "best practice so far" flipped-mastery classroom model.

This book shows you the evolution of their thinking. They share not only what went well, but what they also ultimately decided was not good practice. They want you to learn from their mistakes so that you can make new mistakes and then share what you've learned to improve the model for all. It's both a philosophical look at why they believe the flipped approach is good for learners, and a very practical book describing step-by-step how to get started and what questions you need to consider.

Jon and Aaron describe how their flipped-mastery approach helps their students learn the content better, as well as helps them become better learners. Not only do they score well on tests, but they truly understand chemistry at a much deeper level. Jon and Aaron also describe how it has allowed them to interact more often with their students, how they develop better and more personal relationships with their students, and how students can better personalize their own learning.

For anyone interested in learning more about flipping their classroom, Jon and Aaron have provided a book that helps answer both the "why" and the "how-to." They will help you decide whether you want to flip your classroom (not everyone will). And, if you do decide to flip, they will save you (and your students) countless hours. Not that it will be easy—teaching never is. However, this book quickly gets you up to speed on the potential and the pitfalls of the flipped approach.

Is the flipped approach best for your students? Only you can decide that. But this book is an invaluable aid in helping you do that. Read it. Question it. Try it. Improve on it. Share what you've learned. That's what Jon and Aaron have done with this book.

Karl Fisch

September 2011
Highlands Ranch, Colorado, USA

Chapter 1

OUR STORY:

Creating THE
Flipped Classroom

Enrique is struggling in school, specifically in his math course. Every day his teacher stands in front of the class and teaches to the state standards. She uses the latest technology. She received a grant for an interactive whiteboard that is supposed to engage all kids and get them excited about learning. Enrique's problem is that the teacher talks too fast for him, and he can't take notes quickly enough. When he does get all the notes from class onto paper, he does not understand what they mean. When he goes home to complete his homework, he continues to struggle because what he wrote down in class during the lecture doesn't seem to match with what he is supposed to do on his assignment. Thus, Enrique, a hard-working student, has few options: he can go into class early and ask his teacher for help, he can call a friend with the hope that the friend understood what she said, he can copy the homework from a friend, or he might simply give up.

Janice is active in volleyball, basketball, and track at Eastside High School. She is a conscientious student who always wants to do her best. Unfortunately, she has a difficult science class the last period of every day. She must often leave school early to travel to games and matches, and she misses a lot of classes. She tries to keep up with her science class, but she just can't because she misses so much of it. She sometimes comes in and meets with her teacher before school, but he is often too busy to individually teach her everything she missed.

Ashley has spent the better part of her life learning how to "play school." She is 10 years into mastering the art of meeting her teachers' requirements by making sure that she meets every detail of a grading rubric. She never actually absorbs the key concepts. She consistently earns As and Bs in her classes—not because she has demonstrated understanding, but because she has met the requirements in the rubric. Those grades do not accurately reflect what she has actually learned. Ashley is being served very poorly by her school.

Sadly, these scenarios are common across the country. Many struggling students who genuinely want to learn fall behind instead. Others are so busy that they miss out on key concepts. Still others learn how to "play school," but never really learn important objectives in their courses.

The flipped classroom can address the needs of students such as Enrique, Janice, and Ashley by allowing their teachers to personalize the students' education. You can do the same—whether you teach math, science, social studies, language arts, physical education, ELL, a foreign language, or humanities. This book will show you how!

Background

In 2006, we both started teaching at Woodland Park High School in Woodland Park, Colorado. Jonathan came from Denver and Aaron from southern California. We became the chemistry department at our school of 950 students. As our friendship developed, we realized that we had very similar philosophies of education. To make our lives easier, we began planning our chemistry lessons together, and to save time we divided up much of the work. Aaron would set up one lab and Jonathan the next. Aaron would write the first test, and Jonathan the next.

A problem we noticed right away about teaching in a relatively rural school is that many students miss a great deal of school because of sports and activities. The "nearby" schools are not truly nearby. Students spend an inordinate amount of time on buses traveling to and from events. Thus, students missed our classes and struggled to stay caught up.

And then one day our world changed. Aaron was thumbing through a technology magazine and showed Jonathan an article about some software that would record a PowerPoint slide show, including voice and any annotations, and then convert the recording into a video file that could be easily distributed online. YouTube was just getting started, and the world of online video was in its infancy. But as we discussed the potential of such software, we realized that this might be a way to keep our students who missed class from missing out on learning. So, in the spring of 2007, we began to record our live lessons using screen capture software. We posted our lectures online so our students could access them.

In all honesty, we recorded our lessons out of selfishness. We were spending inordinate amounts of time reteaching lessons to students who missed class, and the recorded lectures became our first line of defense. The conversation usually went something like this:

Student: Mr. Sams, I was gone last class. What did I miss?

Mr. Sams: I tell you what, go to my website, watch the video I posted, and come see me with any questions you have.

Student: OK.

Our absent students loved the recorded lectures. Students who missed class were able to learn what they had missed. Some students who were in class and heard the live lecture began to rewatch the videos. Some would watch them when reviewing for exams. And we loved it because we didn't have to spend hours after school, at lunch, or during our planning time getting kids caught up.

We never could have expected the side effects of posting our lessons online: the emails began. Because our videos were posted online, students and teachers from all over the world began thanking us for them. Students just like ours who had struggled with chemistry found our videos and started using them to learn. We participate in several online science teacher forums, and we began to share the links to the recorded lectures there. Teachers from all over the country began to take notice. Chemistry teachers began to use our video lectures as plans for substitute teachers, and some new teachers used them to learn chemistry content so they could teach it to their students. All in all, it was amazing to see that what we were doing in our small town was being noticed across the country.

The Flipped Classroom Is Born

In our combined total of 37 years of teaching, we have been frustrated with students not being able to translate content from our lectures into useful information that would allow them to complete their homework. Then, one day, Aaron had an insight that would change our world. It was one simple observation: "The time when students really need me physically present is when they get stuck and need my individual help. They don't need me there in the room with them to yak at them and give them content; they can receive content on their own."

He then asked this question: "What if we prerecorded *all* of our lectures, students viewed the video as 'homework,' and then we used the entire class period to help students with the concepts they don't understand?"

Thus, our flipped classroom was born. We made a commitment during the 2007–08 school year to prerecord all of our chemistry and Advanced Placement (AP) chemistry lectures. To make things easier on us, one of us would do Unit 1 of chemistry and the other Unit 1 of AP chemistry. Then we switched off for each subsequent unit. This meant many early mornings for Jonathan, the morning person, and many late nights for Aaron, the night person in our duo.

Our students are on a block schedule where we see them for 95 minutes every other day. Every other night our students watch one of our videos as homework and take notes on what they learned. Teaching science courses, we continued to conduct the same laboratory experiments that we had always done. We found that we had more time for both the labs and the problem work time. In fact, for the first time in either of our careers, we ran out of things for the students to do. They were completing all their work with 20 minutes left in class. Clearly, this model was more efficient than lecturing and assigning homework.

We also decided to give the same end-of-unit tests as we had done the previous year. We discuss the details in the next chapter—but, in short, our students learned more and we had some rough data that seemed to indicate the flipped classroom was a better model than the traditional approach.

We implemented the flipped model for one year and we were very pleased with how our students were learning. We had evidence our model worked and was better for kids. So you would think we would perfect this model and continue to teach that way—but you'd be partially wrong. More on that in a bit.

Before we proceed with our story, we would be remiss if we did not mention a few important facts: (1) We did not lecture exclusively in our classes before flipping; we have always included inquiry-based learning and projects. (2) We were not the first educators to use screencast videos in the classroom as an instructional tool, but we were early adopters and outspoken proponents of the tool, and for us, the flipped class would not have been possible without them. However, there are teachers who use many of the concepts you will read in this book and who call their classrooms flipped, but do not use videos as instructional tools. (3) We did not come up with the term *flipped classroom*. No one owns that term. Although it has been popularized by various media outlets and seems to have stuck, there is no such thing as *the* flipped classroom.

How Flipping Aids Personalization

Flipping the classroom establishes a framework that ensures students receive a personalized education tailored to their individual needs. Remember Enrique, Janice, and Ashley from our opening story? They represent the struggling students, the over-scheduled students, and the students who get by with superficial learning. Educators are expected to find a way to reach these students with their very different needs. Personalization of education has been proposed as a solution.

The movement toward personalization has much merit, but for a single teacher to personalize education for 150 students is difficult and does not work in the traditional educational setting. The present model of education reflects the age in which it was designed: the industrial revolution. Students are educated in an assembly line to make their standardized education efficient. They are asked to sit in nice neat rows, listen to an "expert" expound on a subject, and recall the learned information on an exam. Yet somehow, in this climate, all students are expected to receive the same education. The weakness of the traditional approach is that not all students come to class prepared to learn.

Some lack adequate background for the material, are uninterested in the subject, or have simply been disenchanted with the present educational model.

For the better part of a decade, educators have been told to provide a personalized education for each student, and most educators believe that personalization is a positive goal to reach for each student. However, the logistics of personalizing 150 different educations each day seems insurmountable to most teachers. Exactly how can a teacher personalize the education of so many kids? How can she ensure that every student learns when there are so many standards to cover? Personalization is truly overwhelming for most educators, and they end up taking the shotgun approach to teaching: present as much content as they can in the time they have, and hope that it hits as many students as possible—and sticks.

When we began flipping our classrooms, we quickly realized that we had stumbled on a framework that enables teachers to effectively personalize the education of each student—the goal of educators since the concept of individualized learning first appeared. As we present our flipped classroom model to educators around the world, many have said, "This is reproducible, scalable, customizable, and easy for teachers to wrap their minds around."

You may also have noticed some similarities between a flipped classroom and other educational models such as blended learning, reverse instruction, inverted classroom, and 24/7 classroom. All of these models have similar features and could possibly be interchangeable in certain contexts.

The Flipped Classroom Grows

As we began this journey, we had no idea that what we were doing was going to spread beyond our four walls. Then, out of the blue, we got an email from a neighboring school district wanting us to come and tell them about the flipped model.

They even offered to pay us! So we packed our bags and spent a day in Cañon City, Colorado. Most teachers have sat in staff development training where the principal or superintendent has brought in some "expert"—someone from out of town with a slide show. Well, we were those experts. When we started most of the teachers were sitting there with glazed expressions, as if they were daring these two yahoos to capture their attention.

As we shared our story, their slumped bodies began to become straighter. Soon the teachers in the audience were asking questions and showing genuine interest in the flipped model. And then as we broke them into groups to begin practicing how to make their own videos, we realized we had stumbled on something that was much bigger than ourselves. One seasoned teacher told us that in 26 years of teaching, our presentation and workshop was the most valuable professional development day he had ever attended. I do not know if his comment had as much to do with our presentation skills as it did with the simplicity and reproducibility of the model we presented.

A few weeks later, our assistant principal came into our rooms and asked us, were we expecting anybody from Channel 11? Much to our surprise, the education reporter from one of the news stations had heard about us and had just shown up on our doorstep. The reporter made a short news clip about what we were doing. The rest is history. We were invited to speak at conferences, asked to train educators at schools, districts, and even colleges, and spoke about the flipped classroom across the United States, Canada, and Europe.

The Flipped Mastery Class Begins

Then, one day, our world was rocked by conversations with some of our students. At the end of every year we give students a comprehensive project. In this project, they are asked to analyze a household substance and chemically determine some quantitative property of that substance. The year we implemented the flipped model, students were supposed to analyze a soft drink and determine the percentage of phosphoric acid in the beverage. We have done this project for years, and we were expecting that this group of students, the first who had learned in the flipped model, would set a new standard for good results. When students finish this project, each group has an oral interview with the teacher. In that interview, we ask some key conceptual questions that get to the heart of what students should have learned in chemistry. We were surprised and disappointed to find that, although this group of students had performed better on tests than students in the past, some of their responses in the interview made it seem that they had learned just for the test, instead of really mastering the essential concepts all chemistry students should learn.

On further reflection, we determined that despite our best efforts to meet the needs of all students, we were still pushing our kids through our curriculum whether they were ready to move on or not. We began to wonder if we could set up a flipped classroom that also had elements of a mastery-learning environment (students learning a series of objectives at their own pace). Our conversation went something like this: In the traditional flipped model (It feels strange to say that there is a "traditional" flipped model!), all students watch the same video on the same night. Then, in class, all students complete the same activity or lab. But now that we have a library of instructional videos, why does every student need to be on the same topic at the same time?

Another thing that got us thinking about the flipped-mastery model was the entrance of a foreign exchange student into Jonathan's class. The counselors came to Jonathan and asked him if a student could join his chemistry class at the beginning of the second semester. When Jonathan asked about her previous chemistry class, he was told that she had no background. Before we made our videos, there would have been no way to allow such a student into class in the middle of the year. As Jonathan thought it through, he realized that he had a whole library of videos made for chemistry. She could work through them at her own pace. He took the student into his class. She started at Unit 1 and worked her way through the chemistry curriculum. In our course we have 10 units that cover the entire year. She got through 8 of the 10 in one semester. As we observed her work, we began to think about a system where all students worked through the material as they mastered the content at their own pace.

Our ultimate goal is for all students to really learn chemistry. We wondered if we could set up a system in which students progress through the course as they master the material. You must understand that we had never been trained in how to implement a mastery system of learning. Subsequently, we discovered that mastery learning has been around for a long time. A great deal of research has been done on how to implement such a system. We didn't consult the literature, we didn't do any research: we simply jumped in.

Our first year of teaching with the flipped-mastery model was a year with a steep learning curve. We made a lot of mistakes. When that year was over, we looked at each other and asked, "Should we continue with this?" Both of us realized that we could not go back. We had seen our students learning chemistry more deeply than ever before, and we were convinced. Our method was changing students' abilities to become self-directed learners.

Are You Ready to Flip?

By now you may have realized that we have a pretty high tolerance for change. We are willing to try almost anything if we think it will help our students. And fortunately, we have made many good decisions along the journey. We have also made many mistakes. It is our hope that if you decide to implement the flipped or even the flipped-mastery model, you will learn from our mistakes and improve on our model.

We also hope that as you read, you realize that there is no single way to flip your classroom—there is no such thing as *the* flipped classroom. There is no specific methodology to be replicated, no checklist to follow that leads to guaranteed results. Flipping the classroom is more about a mindset: redirecting attention away from the teacher and putting attention on the learner and the learning. Every teacher who has chosen to flip does so differently. In fact, even though we developed our flipped class together and are next door to each other, Jonathan's classroom still looks different from Aaron's classroom, and our personalities and individual teaching styles shine through the commonalities.

We purposely kept this book short, hoping you will read it in one sitting, or at most over a weekend. It is organized quite simply: first the flipped classroom, then the flipped-mastery model, and finally a section with FAQs and concluding thoughts. We answer the questions of what, why, and how to implement each model. Also interspersed throughout the book are anecdotes and quotes from other educators across the globe who have in some fashion flipped their classrooms.

Chapter 2

THE
Flipped Classroom

At this point you should have an idea of what a flipped class entails, but you may be asking exactly what in the classroom is "flipped." Basically the concept of a flipped class is this: that which is traditionally done in class is now done at home, and that which is traditionally done as homework is now completed in class. But as you will see, there is more to a flipped classroom than this.

We are often asked about what the flipped classroom looks like on a day-to-day basis. Essentially, we start each class with a few minutes of discussion about the video from the night before. One of the drawbacks to the flipped model is that students cannot ask immediate questions that come to their mind, as they could if the topic were being taught live. To address this issue, we spend a considerable amount of time at the beginning of the year training the students to view our videos effectively. We encourage them to turn off iPods, phones, and other distractions while they watch the video. We then teach them that they now have the ability to "pause" and "rewind" their teacher. We encourage them to liberally use the pause button so they can write down key points of the lesson. In addition, we instruct them in the Cornell note-taking method, in which they take notes, record any questions they have, and summarize their learning. Students who adopt this model of note taking typically come to class with appropriate questions that help us address their misconceptions. We also use these questions to evaluate the effectiveness of our videos. If every student has a similar question, we clearly did not teach that topic well, and we make a note to remake or correct that particular video.

After the initial questions are answered, students are given the assignment for the day. It might be a lab, an inquiry activity, a directed problem-solving activity, or a test. Because we are on a 95-minute block schedule, students usually do more than one of these activities in any given class period.

We continue to grade assignments, labs, and tests just as we always have under the traditional model. But the role of the teacher in the classroom has dramatically changed. We are no longer the presenters of information; instead, we take on more of a tutorial role. The change experienced by the teacher was probably identified best by Shari Kendrick, a teacher in San Antonio who adopted our model: "I don't have to go to school and perform five times a day. Instead I spend my days interacting with and helping my students." One huge benefit of flipping is that the students who struggle get the most help. We spend our time walking around the room helping students with concepts they are stuck on.

In the traditional model, students would usually come into class confused about some of the homework problems from the previous night. Generally we would spend the first 25 minutes doing a warm-up activity and going over those problems they didn't understand. We would then present new content for 30 to 45 minutes and spend the remainder of the class with indepen-dent practice or a lab.

In the flipped model, the time is completely restructured. Students still need to ask questions about the content that has been delivered via video, so we generally answer these questions during the first few minutes of class. This allows us to clear up misconceptions before they are practiced and applied incorrectly. The remainder of the time is used for more extensive hands-on activities and/or directed problem-solving time (see Table 2.1).

TABLE 2.1 Comparison of Class Time in Traditional versus Flipped Classrooms

Traditional Classroom		Flipped Classroom	
Activity	*Time*	*Activity*	*Time*
Warm-up activity	5 min.	Warm-up activity	5 min.
Go over previous night's homework	20 min.	Q&A time on video	10 min.
Lecture new content	30–45 min.	Guided and independent practice and/or lab activity	75 min.
Guided and independent practice and/or lab activity	20–35 min.		

Let's look at a typical unit in Aaron's AP chemistry class and see an example of how the role of the teacher has changed.

Aaron's AP chemistry class begins the night before in the home of each student. Students are not assigned problems or reading from the book, but rather, a video. All students will watch a video (on their iPod, computer, or TV) of Aaron and Jonathan explaining the material that will be applied in class in the morning.

Class begins. Aaron quickly takes attendance and starts a question-and-answer session. Students ask questions about the previous night's video, and Aaron helps clarify misconceptions. After 10 minutes or so, Aaron instructs the students to take out their packet of practice problems, many of which are similar in structure to the type of questions they will see on the AP Chemistry exam. He leads the class through a few examples that reflect the content students learned the night before and takes any further questions. Then it is time to work. The students complete the remaining assigned problems while Aaron moves around the class helping students as they have questions. A solution guide is available to students who want to check their work.

On days when a lab will be conducted, no video is assigned. Instead, students complete a prelab activity at home. In class, Aaron fields any pertinent questions about the lab and discusses safety. Then the students begin experimenting. Under a traditional model, the completion of any calculations and discussions is usually assigned as homework after a lab. Under the flipped classroom model, however, the next video is assigned for homework, and students are given time in class the next day to complete the lab. This allows Aaron to answer specific questions about the lab and assist struggling students with their calculations, as well as discuss the data collected as a class.

When exam day rolls around, all students take the exam at the same time and are provided timely feedback so misconceptions can be addressed. Ultimately, all students need to be through the curriculum by the end of April so preparation can be made for the AP exam in May. So that all students are prepared for the exam by the established date, they all work at the same pace.

Clearly, the class is centered around the students and not the teacher. Students are responsible for viewing the videos and asking appropriate questions. The teacher is simply there to provide expert feedback. The students are responsible for completing and sharing their work. Because a solution guide is available, students are motivated to learn, not just to complete the assignments in a rote manner. Students are responsible for making appropriate use of the resident expert to help them understand the concepts. The role of the teacher in the classroom is to help students, not to deliver information.

Teaching under a traditional model is draining. I feel like I have to "perform," which requires energy, enthusiasm, and a "you are on-stage" effort at all times. I remember last year driving into work, thinking, "Man, I feel like just being a student today. I wish I could go in and let someone else do all the work—be in the passenger seat for once." When I switched over I felt *free*. I was able to go in and watch my students work. I don't mean that I sat back and drank coffee—I stayed busy interacting one-on-one; working with kids who were struggling; addressing questions that students had that I never had time for before; really getting to know my kids. It is just that the burden of learning had traded hands. And you know, really, it had to be passed on. I can't force someone to learn—they have to accept that responsibility for themselves. This method allows them to clearly see that—and gives them a struc-tured environment that ensures success.

— JENNIFER DOUGLASS (WESTSIDE HIGH SCHOOL,
    MACON, GEORGIA)

Chapter 3

Why
You Should Flip
YOUR Classroom

Flipping the classroom has transformed our teaching practice. We no longer stand in front of our students and talk at them for 30 to 60 minutes at a time. This radical change has allowed us to take on a different role with our students. Both of us taught for many years using a lecture format. We were both good teachers. In fact, Jonathan received the Presidential Award for Excellence in Math and Science Teaching as a lecturer, and Aaron received the same award under the flipped model. As we look back, however, we realize we could never go back to teaching in the traditional manner.

The flipped classroom has changed not just our own classrooms. Teachers from around the world have adopted the model and are using it to teach classes in all curriculum areas to elementary, middle, and high school students as well as adults. We have seen how flipping your classroom can change kids' lives. In this chapter, we want to highlight why you should consider flipping your classroom.

I can't think of a reason to willingly go back to the traditional lecture method. I have to teach so many different courses this year that I have not been able to use the video/mastery method in my forensics course. I hate teaching it, because I now hate lecturing.

— BRETT WILIE (FIRST BAPTIST ACADEMY, DALLAS, TEXAS)

Flipping speaks the language of today's students

Today's students grew up with Internet access, YouTube, Facebook, MySpace, and a host of other digital resources. They can typically be found doing their math homework while texting their friends, IMing on Facebook, and listening to music all at the same time. Many of these students report that when they come to school, they have to turn off and dumb down because their schools ban cell phones, iPods, and any other digital devices. The sad thing is that most students are carrying in their pockets a more powerful computing device than the vast majority of computers in our underfunded schools—and we don't allow them to use it.

When we present the flipped classroom to educators, we usually get an *ooh-ahh* reaction from our audiences, which are primarily made up of adults who did not grow up with the always-on digital world. When we began flipping, we were surprised at our students' lack of amazement. After about two weeks of watching the videos, they had settled into learning, and the "wow" factor was gone. These students understand digital learning. To them, all we are doing is speaking their language. Don't get us wrong—we are not saying they don't appreciate learning this way. But instruction via video is not a big deal for today's students.

One concern we have heard from adults is that we're increasing screen time in front of a computer, which aggravates the disconnect many adults feel with today's youth. To that we say that we are infiltrating the video/digital culture instead of fighting it. Isn't it about time we embraced digital learning and used it to help our students learn, instead of telling them they can't learn with today's tools? It seems preposterous to us that schools have not embraced this change.

When you walk into our classrooms, you will see students engaged in a variety of activities using different digital devices. Students are working on our (obsolete) class computers, they are using their iPods, they are working together, they are experimenting, and they are interacting with their teacher. We encourage our students to bring in their own electronic equipment because, frankly, it is better than our school's antiquated technology.

Bad Reasons for Flipping Your Classroom

Because some guys who got a book published told you to.

We're flattered that you are interested in what we have to say, but do not adopt any teaching strategy without thinking it through first.

Because you think it will create a 21st-century classroom.

Pedagogy should always drive technology, never the other way around.

Because you think you will become cutting edge.

Flipping does not necessarily use the latest technology.

Because you think flipping your classroom exempts you from being a good teacher.

Teaching is much more than good content delivery.

Because you think it will make your job easier.

Flipping will *not* make your job any easier.

Flipping helps busy students

Students today are busy, busy, busy. Many are overprogrammed, going from one event to the next. Our students appreciate the flexibility of the flipped classroom. Because the main content is delivered via online videos, students can choose to work ahead. Jonathan had a student who was a competitive gymnast who regularly traveled to out-of-state competitions. When she was gone, she missed most of the instruction in her classes. But because she was in a flipped classroom for science, she did not miss any of the content in that class. She chose to work ahead when competitions were coming up. When she returned, she had at least one class she didn't have to worry about.

Aaron had a student who is heavily involved in student council. This year, when homecoming was approaching, she worked ahead. She got one week ahead in his class, and when homecoming week happened, she used Aaron's class time to work on homecoming activities. These two students have not just learned how to "work the system"—they are learning valuable life lessons in managing their time. This would not work in a traditional classroom, but flipping the classroom provides a great deal of flexibility to help students with their busy lives.

> We have students that travel very far to get to school (some up to an hour and a half on the subway each way) and this allows them to work on chemistry whenever they want. Many of my students also participate in multiple sports, so athletes are not missing class anymore, which helps everyone in the long run.
>
> — BRIAN BENNETT (AN INTERNATIONAL SCHOOL IN SEOUL, SOUTH KOREA)

Flipping helps struggling students

When we taught in the traditional manner, the students who tended to get most of our attention were the best and brightest—students who would raise their hands first and ask great questions. In the meantime, the rest of the students would passively listen to the conversation we had with the inquisitive students. But since our introduction of the flipped model, our role has changed; we spend most of our class walking around helping the students who struggle most. We think this may be the single most important reason students thrive in the flipped model. This is not to say that we ignore our top students. But the majority of our attention no longer goes to them. Now it is directed to the students who need the most help.

Flipping helps students of all abilities to excel

Our special education teachers love this model as well. Because all the direct instruction is recorded, students with special needs can watch the videos as many times as they need to learn the material. No more frantically trying to copy down notes with the hope that they'll understand them later. Instead, students can pause their teacher, rewind their teacher, and make sure they actually learn the important concepts.

Some of the students that have struggled in the past (according to their parents) are doing much better because of my ability to work with them more one-on-one in class, helping with objectives they are having trouble with.

— BRETT WILIE (FIRST BAPTIST ACADEMY, DALLAS, TEXAS)

Flipping allows students to pause and rewind their teacher

As educators, we usually have a specific curriculum we need to cover in our courses. Students are expected to learn a given body of knowledge, and most of the time we hope that they understand our presentations. However, even the best presenters and lecturers have students who fall behind and don't understand or learn all that is required. When we flipped the classroom, we gave the students control of the remote. Giving students the ability to pause their teachers is truly revolutionary.

Jonathan's daughter was in one of his classes, and while Jonathan observed her watching one of the videos at home, she suddenly burst out and said, "I love these videos." He asked her why. She said, "I can pause you!"

Pausing is a powerful feature for a number of reasons. Making students all sit in tidy rows and listen to their teacher eloquently explain his or her area of expertise is not always an effective means of communicating to them. We often move too fast for some students and too slowly for others. Our quick learners understand immediately and get bored waiting, while our struggling students take more time to process. Inevitably, when we click the arrow to move to the next slide, a small group of students scream and shout asking to go back to the previous slide. When we give students the ability to pause their teachers, they have the chance to process at the speed that is appropriate for them. We especially encourage students who process more slowly to use the rewind button so they can hear us explain something more than one time. If they still don't understand, we will work with them individually or in small groups in the classroom.

On the other end, we have students who are often bored because the teacher is going too slowly for them. These students appreciate the pause function for different reasons. These typically are our busiest students, involved in myriad activities and sports.

Giving them the ability to pause helps these students with time management. Jonathan's daughter was one of these students, and she liked the pause button so she could break up the lesson into shorter segments and learn on her own schedule. We even have had a few students who watch our videos at double speed. These students are able to process our instruction faster than most, and though our voices sound as if we have been inhaling helium, they find this to be a better use of their time.

Flipping increases student–teacher interaction

A statement we frequently hear goes something like this: "This is a great method for online teaching, but I don't want to replace my classroom with online courses." Though flipping certainly has great potential to change online education, the purpose of this book is not to promote the benefits of such education. We are both classroom teachers who see our students every day. Most students today still come to a brick-and-mortar school where they see both their teachers and their peers.

We believe that flipping allows teachers to leverage technology to increase interaction with students. We must be clear, however. We are not advocating the replacement of classrooms and classroom teachers with online instruction. In fact, we strongly believe that flipping the classroom creates an ideal merger of online and face-to-face instruction that is becoming known as a "blended" classroom. We often conduct minilectures with groups of students who are struggling with the same content. The beauty of these minilectures is we are delivering just-in-time instruction when the students are ready for learning.

Teachers play a vital role in the lives of their students. They are mentors, friends, neighbors, and experts. Having face-to-face interaction with teachers is an invaluable experience for students.

I wanted to thank you and Aaron for turning me on to the flipped classroom. I was observed by one of the assistant principals and he loved the idea so much he went to the principal later that day and told him everything I was doing. He said that every administrator should see this model and I seem to be the only one implementing all aspects of the philosophy of the school. He wants me to conduct a professional development workshop on it for next year so more teachers can start doing this.

So, being a nontenured teacher in a district in a budget crisis, I think you helped me secure a job for life. Thank you so much for the work you two have done and how you have inspired me to take my teaching to the next level. One day I will have to make it out to Colorado to thank you in person.

— MARC SEIGEL (BASKING RIDGE, NEW JERSEY)

Flipping allows teachers to know their students better

We as teachers are at school not only to teach content, but also to inspire, to encourage, to listen, and to provide a vision for our students. This happens in the context of relationships. We have always believed that a good teacher builds relationships with students. Students need positive adult role models in their lives. We hope we can be such role models. We developed these relationships before we flipped the classroom, but flipping allows us to build better relationships with our students.

This is due to the increased teacher-student interaction. The year we started flipping, we encouraged students to interact with us via text messaging. Most of the time the content of these text messages is along the lines of "How do I get help on problem X?" or "What is the benchmark for this coming week?" Because we make the instructional videos together, most of our students do not think of Jonathan or Aaron as their teacher—they think of both of us as their teachers. Naturally, some students connect better with Aaron and some better with Jonathan. One day one of Aaron's students started texting Jonathan, and at first, the texts were all about science. Soon the tone of the texts changed. Jonathan realized this student was calling out for help and referred him to our counseling staff. As it turned out, this student had been kicked out of his house and was going through some intense personal issues. Though flipping didn't create this relationship, it helped create a positive environment where the struggling student could interact with an adult, and this student got the help he needed.

Flipping increases student–student interaction

One of the greatest benefits of flipping is that overall interaction increases: teacher-to-student, and student-to-student. Because the role of the teacher has changed from presenter of content to learning coach, we spend our time talking to kids. We are answering questions, working with small groups, and guiding the learning of each student individually.

When students are working on an assignment and we notice that several of them are struggling with the same thing, we spontaneously organize these students into a tutorial group.

Because the role of the teacher has changed to more of a tutor than a deliverer of content, we have the privilege of observing as students interact with each other. As we roam around the class, we notice the students developing their own collaborative groups. Students are helping each other learn instead of relying on the teacher as the sole disseminator of knowledge. It is truly magical to observe. We are often in awe of how well our students work together and learn from each other.

Some might ask how we developed a culture of learning. We think the key is for students to identify learning as their goal, instead of striving for the completion of assignments. We have purposely tried to make our classes places where students carry out meaningful activities instead of completing busywork. When we respect our students in this way, they usually respond. They begin to realize—and for some it takes time—that we are here to guide them in their learning instead of being authoritative pedagogues. Our goal is for them to be the best learners possible, and to truly understand the content in our classes. When our students grasp the concept that we are on their side, they respond by doing their best.

Flipping allows for real differentiation

One of the struggles in today's schools is accommodating a vast range of abilities in each class. We have everyone from students who excel, to average students, to students who struggle with our content, to students who cannot read. Flipping the class showed us just how needy many of our students were and how powerful the flipped classroom is in reaching students all along this broad range of abilities.

Because the majority of our time is used to walk around the room and help students, we can personalize the learning of all. For our students who quickly understand the content, we have found that if they can prove to us their understanding of a particular objective, we will cut down on the number of problems they need to do. Think of these as individual contracts with each student, where the student has to prove understanding. These students appreciate this because they realize we are not interested in busywork, but rather learning.

For our students who struggle, we look for key understanding. We realize that our course is hard for many students and that learning doesn't come easily for all. For these students, we often modify their work on the fly by asking them to complete only key problems instead of all of them. This way our students who struggle will learn the essential objectives and not get bogged down with some of the more advanced topics that may just confuse them.

During my time in undergrad and graduate school, I heard about how students do not all learn the same way, or at the same pace. These classes introduced the concept of a differentiated classroom, but I never knew how I could actually do that when there was only one of me, and 25–30 students in the class needing me to teach 12 different lessons to them. When I heard about creating instructional video clips, I finally realized that this is what I need in order to be able to create 25 copies of myself … which would allow kids the freedom to speed up, or slow down, as needed. I also was incredibly frustrated with students taking quizzes and tests unprepared, doing poorly, and then we would move on—regardless of performance. Now I can use classroom time to address student questions and review problems that they are frequently missing.

— MELISSA DE JONG (ROOSEVELT HIGH SCHOOL, SIOUX FALLS, SOUTH DAKOTA)

Flipping changes classroom management

Under a traditional model of teaching, we had students who consistently did not pay attention in class. These students were often a distraction to the rest of the class and negatively affected everybody else's learning. They were often either bored or just simply unruly. When we flipped the classroom, we discovered something amazing. Because we were not just standing and talking *at* kids, many of the classroom management problems evaporated. Students who needed an audience no longer had one. Because class time is primarily used for students to either do hands-on activities or work in small groups, those students who were typically a distraction become a nonissue. They either did not have an audience or they were no longer bored and were willing to dive into the learning.

Don't get us wrong. We still have to redirect students. We still have students who underperform. But so many of the bigger classroom management issues have simply disappeared.

Flipping changes the way we talk to parents

We both remember years of sitting in parent conferences, where parents would often ask us how their son or daughter behaved in class. What they were really asking was, "Does my child sit quietly, act respectfully, raise his or her hand, and not disturb other students?" These skills are certainly good for all to learn—but when we first started flipping the classroom, we struggled to answer this question.

You see, the question is a nonissue in our classroom. Because students are coming with the primary focus on learning, there are two real questions now: Is each student learning? If not, what can we do to help them learn? These are much more profound questions, and when we discuss them with parents, we move the focus to a place that will help parents understand how their students can become better learners.

There are myriad reasons why a student may not be learning well. The student may have some missing background knowledge. The student may have personal issues that interfere with learning. Or the student may be more concerned with "playing school" than actually learning. When we (the parents and teachers) can diagnose why the child is not learning, we create a powerful moment where the necessary interventions can be implemented.

Flipping educates parents

A surprising thing happened when we started talking to parents during parent teacher conferences. Many of them told us they loved our videos. We then asked, "You watch our videos?" As it turns out, many of them were watching right alongside their children and learning science. This leads to interesting discussions between students and parents about the content of our lessons. This has been echoed across the country as other teachers have adopted our model. They have told us similar stories of educating their parent community.

At a conference we attended a few years ago, one of the keynote speakers was a kindergarten teacher who told us this story. She taught in an ethnically diverse school that had many new English-language learners. One of the key ingredients in becoming a good reader is to be read to. She was awarded a grant for some iPod Nanos on which she recorded herself, and others, reading books to her students. The ELL students would then take the iPod Nanos home with the corresponding book and would listen to the story read to them.

As the iPods were continually being used by students she started noticing they were coming back to her with the batteries almost drained. She knew how long the batteries would last and expressed her puzzlement with her students. When parent-teacher conferences occurred, one mother told her she was sorry for draining the batteries of the iPod. The mother then told this teacher that not only was she listening to the stories, but so were the grandmother, the aunt, and the whole extended family. The teacher's audio files were educating many more people than she ever expected.

I have had *very* positive feedback from parents. Flipping the classroom has enabled parents to help their children because the parents are watching the videos too. A few of them thought that I was no longer teaching, and it took a bit to dispel this notion, but then they began to see how much more I was working one-on-one with their children with this method.

— BRETT WILIE (FIRST BAPTIST ACADEMY, DALLAS, TEXAS)

Flipping makes your class transparent

In this age where a segment of our communities distrust the educational establishment, flipping opens the doors to our class-rooms and allows the public in. Our videos are posted on the

Internet, and our students' parents and others have free access to them. Instead of wondering what their students are being exposed to in the classroom, parents can find our lessons in just a few clicks.

Like it or not, schools are competing for students. Our school loses some students to neighboring schools for a variety of reasons. Much of our loss has been because parents incorrectly perceive our school to be less academic than nearby schools. Posting our videos and opening our instructional practices to the public has brought some of these students back to our school.

Flipping is a great technique for absent teachers

We teach in a semirural school where it is hard to obtain qualified substitute teachers. We especially have a hard time getting qualified teachers to walk into a chemistry class. When we first started recording our lessons and posting the videos online, we simply recorded our lessons live in front of our students. It then dawned on us that we could prerecord a lesson for our students ahead of time when we knew we were going to be gone. Jonathan was headed to a wedding out of town and thought he would try this out. He sat down in front of his computer and recorded the lesson he would normally have given. The substitute plan was simply to turn on the LCD projector, pull up the video file, and press Play. Students took notes as if he were there in class. This way his students didn't miss a beat. They got the same lesson on the right day. Students reported how almost eerie it was to hear Jonathan's voice without him being present in the class.

This method is being used across the country. An elementary teacher in our district, when gone, prerecords his lessons for his students. Doing so ensures that students are taught the way he wants them to be taught, and he does not have to reteach on his return. The substitutes appreciate this method of teaching because students are getting just what the teacher wants. We even know of science teachers across the country using our videos as the substitute plans when they are gone.

Flipping can lead to the flipped-mastery program

This chapter has been a bit awkward for us to write because we no longer just flip our classrooms. Instead we are using the flipped-mastery model, in which students move through the material at their own pace. No longer do all students watch the same video on the same night. Students watch and learn in an asynchronous system where they work toward content mastery. We should note that we did not start using the flipped-mastery program until two years after abandoning the traditional model. Our journey has been a process that has occurred over several years, and we recommend that those interested in flipping make the change gradually.

Chapter 4

How to Implement
THE
Flipped Classroom

In this chapter we address many of the logistics of implementing a flipped classroom including making or finding high-quality videos. We also offer suggestions for flipping your classroom.

Homework: The Videos

Before you jump into video production, carefully consider whether or not a video is the appropriate instructional tool for the desired educational outcome. If a video is appropriate, then proceed with planning one. If a video is not appropriate, then do not make one just for the sake of making a video. Doing so would be a disservice to your students and would be a prime example of "technology for technology's sake." Only employ the technology if it is an appropriate tool for the task at hand. Use your professional judgment, ask your peers and mentors, and even ask your students.

Probably the single most daunting task teachers face when trying to flip the classroom is accessing or producing high-quality videos. We have found teachers who are very comfortable both with technology and with recording themselves. If this describes you, you may want to skip ahead to the Making Your Own Videos section. Others may not have the time to create their own videos, struggle with technology, or do not speak well in front of a computer screen. If this describes you, we encourage you to think about using somebody else's videos as you implement a flipped classroom.

Using Other Teachers' Videos

Using videos produced by other teachers, and not producing your own videos, may be your best option as you begin flipping your classroom. Maybe you want to start flipping, but you just don't have time to produce your own videos. Maybe you're also not very good with talking in front of a screen, or with using the screencasting technology. When we make our videos, we sit in our classroom and talk to the computer and each other. It is harder than teaching in front of a live audience. Students are not present, and thus we have to bring a somewhat artificial dynamic presence. We don't want to bore our students with dry videos, so we make them interesting. Thus, if you find a gifted teacher who has already made videos in your subject, by all means, feel free to use them. Some time ago we started selling our chemistry videos online. Many chemistry teachers who wanted to flip their classrooms simply used our videos and did not produce their own. Others purchased our videos to use them for some of the flipped lessons, using their own videos for the rest. With the explosion of YouTube and other video sharing sites, the number of videos is growing. Many of these videos can be used in a flipped classroom.

The key is to find quality videos regardless of your subject matter. Where do you find good-quality videos? This is not an easy question. Depending on your subject, you may have to look far and long. However, the exponential growth of free online video resources is making the search increasingly easier.

A side benefit that has appeared is that students have figured out they can search online and find recorded lessons from other sources. This is a great learning tool for them in that they are taking responsibility for their own learning and discovering ways to find the information they need. These kids are growing up in a digital world and it is important they learn how to navigate through it and find information they may need on their own.

— BRETT WILIE (FIRST BAPTIST ACADEMY, DALLAS, TEXAS)

Making Your Own Videos

When we use the word *video*, most teachers think of a video camera on them while they teach their class. Although this might be effective in some cases, we believe there are better ways to make videos for use in the flipped classroom. We use a screencasting program, Camtasia Studio, that captures anything on our screen, our voices, a small webcam of our faces, and any digital pen annotations we include. The pen feature is especially useful for lessons that involve mathematical problem solving. Precreating a bunch of numbers to appear on a PowerPoint slide show is not as dynamic as writing with the pen, in real time, and describing our thought process as we explain a problem. Other features, such as picture-in-picture, video clips, and many other postproduction items can be added to improve the quality of the videos.

In this next section we discuss the equipment and steps needed to create a prerecorded video lesson. If you would like to flip your classroom but are concerned about the time commitment for making videos, consider spending one year recording all your live direct instruction. By simply pressing Record before each lesson and Stop at the end, over the course of one year you will build a library of videos. After doing so, you can decide what to do with the videos and how to restructure your class. This method does not require any additional work, comes at a minimal monetary cost, and is the easiest way to head toward a flipped class.

Video-Making Equipment

Our videos are very inexpensive to make. All we have is screencasting software, a computer, a pen-tablet input device, a microphone, and a webcam. Most newer computers today have a microphone and webcam built in, so the only two things you will need to purchase are the pen-tablet input device and the software.

Screencasting software. Screencasting software captures whatever is on your computer screen. If you are showing a PowerPoint presentation, it records the presentation. If you are navigating to a web page, it captures your navigation. If you are annotating on the computer, it will record your pen strokes. When a microphone is set up, it also records voice. There are many different screencasting programs available. Some are free and open source, some are for Windows computers, some for Macintosh, and some for Linux. Presently, we use Camtasia Studio to make our recordings. The key is not to get caught up in which software to use, but rather, to find a program that works for you, in your situation.

Pen annotation. As teachers of a mathematically based science class, we find the pen annotation feature indispensable. We need to be able to write on our screen. The primary software we use is Microsoft PowerPoint. It has a pen annotation feature that we use extensively. We have begun experimenting with SMART software because we recently received SMART boards in our classrooms, but any interactive whiteboard software includes a pen feature.

If your videos require pen annotation, there are quite a few hardware options available. These devices range in price from a very inexpensive USB pen tablet (less than $60) to interactive whiteboards (upwards of $4,000). There are many manufacturers of the tablets, which plug into a computer. One of the most popular examples of such a device is the Wacom Bamboo. The next tier of devices is wireless tablets. These tablets are made by a variety of manufacturers and can be obtained for between $200 and $400. These devices work the same as the wired tablets. We recommend these if teachers are planning on recording some or all of their lessons live. The advantage to a wireless tablet is that you can move around the room as you present content to students.

Teachers can also use a tablet PC. These devices have the pen functionality built in. Frankly, we are not big fans of tablet PCs because you pay extra money for a computer. Jonathan bought his first wireless tablet in 2001. Since then, he has gone through seven computers—yet he still has his original wireless tablet, and it continues to work. If he had originally purchased a tablet PC, he would have had to replace seven tablet PCs, which would have been much more expensive than purchasing one wireless tablet and replacing seven standard PCs.

Interactive whiteboard. Interactive whiteboards are designed for annotation. Many teachers we know use their interactive whiteboards to record their lessons. The only disadvantage to these is that you have to be in your classroom to make the recordings. We like the flexibility of recording at home, in a hotel room in Atlanta, on the National Mall in Washington, D.C., or in the classrooms of colleagues interested in flipping. Some schools that have used interactive whiteboards as their main devices have purchased a few of the USB tablets for teachers to take home to make some of the videos.

Microphone. Microphones also vary in price and functionality. Most newer laptops have built-in microphones. However, in our experience, many of these microphones are not of very high quality. We recommend that you create a recording, play it back, and see what you think. You can also purchase external microphones for under $10 at a local big box retailer. These are not the highest quality, but they work. An advantage to an external microphone is that it won't record the sounds of clicking a mouse or track pad that a built-in microphone will.

When we started recording, we recorded live. We realized we wanted to be mobile as we taught, so we researched wireless options. There are a number of relatively decent wireless microphones that can be obtained for about $50. We found wireless USB headsets that gamers use with the Xbox to work quite well. When we started recording together, we realized the microphones we were using were not going to pick up both of our voices very well. Thus we began to research higher quality microphones. We found a USB microphone that was studio quality and have been very happy with its performance. When we introduced the flipped classroom to our foreign language teachers, they required high sound fidelity to capture appropriate voice inflections and pronunciation. They were not happy with the performance of any of the cheaper microphones and subsequently purchased a higher quality microphone.

Webcam. Most newer laptops come with a built-in webcam, so this is most likely all you need, but you may need to purchase one to add this feature. We regularly use a webcam and the PIP feature to include science demonstrations that are either unsafe or too lengthy to conduct in class. We record our lesson, pause the recording, then turn the webcam onto the science demonstration and resume the recording to capture the event.

Recording software. The recording software we use has a picture-in-picture (PIP) feature we really like. It will capture a webcam shot of the presenter(s) while they record. After recording the session, we can use the editing features to change the size and position of the PIP. At first we wondered if this would be distracting to students, but when we surveyed them, they told us they liked seeing our faces. "You aren't just a disembodied voice talking to us—you're a real person."

Video camera. Once we started experimenting with our webcam, we quickly realized that there is great value in creating more than a screencast. Screencasts form the backbone of our videos, but putting in short clips from a video camera has turned out to be a powerful addition to our videos. We purchased a digital video camera from a big box retailer, and we shoot clips as often as we can. Some of these clips involve scientific experiments: we have set things on fire, and we have zoomed in closely to see scientific phenomena. We also shoot clips whenever and wherever we see science in the world around us. In doing so, we bring the world to our students. When Jonathan was in Peru, his son shot some video of Jonathan explaining the geology of the Andes Mountains. When we were in Washington, D.C., speaking at a conference, we talked about the chemistry of diamonds in front of the Hope Diamond at the Smithsonian.

We did not spend a great deal of money on equipment to begin flipping our classrooms. We started with the tablet, added the software, and then over time upgraded to a better quality microphone, a stand-alone webcam, and eventually a digital video camera. Making your own high-quality videos is no longer expensive. Anybody can create them with minimal expense.

Stages in Making a Video

When we make our videos, there are four stages: planning the lesson, recording the video, editing the video, and then publishing the video.

1. **Planning the lesson.** First determine the objective of your lesson and decide whether a video is an appropriate instructional tool to accomplish the educational goal of the lesson. If a video of direct instruction is not the best tool, then *do not proceed with these steps*. If it is, please continue. Remember, flipping is not just about making videos for your class. Although most educators who have flipped their classes use screencast videos, there are teachers who have implemented all of the educational ideas in this book without using a single video. When we began, we already had a series of PowerPoint files we had used for our lectures for years. We simply recorded video using those same slides, and we recommend that you also begin recording using material you have already created. Early in our flipping adventure, we were not as conscientious about

what should be recorded and what should not. We simply recorded everything we had lectured on in the past. As we have matured in our process, we have begun to eliminate certain videos from our curriculum that are redundant, unnecessary, or ineffective. As you continue making more and more videos, start to alter your existing material to be better suited for a screencast. After a while you will become comfortable with the features of the screencasting software you are using, so plan for those features. For example, if you would like to add video clips, leave blank slides as a mental note and placeholder for clips to be inserted after the fact. If you know you will be working out problems using a digital pen, leave blank slides for writing. If you would like to use a calculator emulator, leave space on slides for the calculator to be displayed. Want to use a webcam? Be sure to have a place on your screen where it will reside. Thus, the more complex your final video product will be, the more you need to plan.

2. **Recording the video.** Recording the lesson entails sitting at your computer or interactive white board with a microphone, webcam, writing device, or document camera. You simply "teach" the lesson to your absent audience, pausing occasionally to plan what will be said next, or to correct a mistake. We have found that some teachers are more comfortable working from a script or outline, and that's fine. However, we do not write a script. This is for two main reasons: (1) our slide show serves as enough of an outline that we, as veteran teachers, can simply improvise adequate conversation to teach the material, and (2) a script would simply hinder our spontaneity and creativity. We prefer our lessons to be more conversational and less formal. Our students have told us that they prefer conversational videos featuring both of us; thus, we make time to create these together to include this dynamic. However, our videos tend to run long, and a script or more focused instruction would lead to a shorter video. As always, know what your students need and give it to them.

3. **Editing the video.** You can do as much or as little editing as you want. When we first recorded our lessons, we did no postproduction editing. We simply recorded our lesson and published it for student use. Eventually, we discovered the added value of postproduction editing, and we now spend considerable time editing. The editing process is time consuming, but it allows the teacher to remove mistakes instead of rerecording an entire video. It also allows the teacher to highlight and reinforce what has been said in the recording with a visual cue that can aid in student understanding. During the editing process you can insert videos, change picture-in-picture settings, zoom in and out to various areas of the screen, and add text callouts (think VH-1 Pop Up Video from the early 1990s). We discuss these video elements in the next section. When commercial film producers make videos, they spend much more time editing than recording. As classroom teachers, we realize we do not have the luxury of spending too much time editing. Although we do edit, we do not go over the top with the amount of time we spend on it. Our editing rule of thumb: Do I need this video perfect, or do I need it Tuesday?

4. **Publishing the video.** Last, publish the video for your students to view. The big question with teachers interested in making their own videos is "Where do I put the videos so all students can view them?" The answer to this question is different for every teacher, school, and district. Every IT department is different, every school acceptable-use policy is different, and how a school makes these available for students will vary. We currently post our videos on an online hosting site, our internal district servers, and locally on the computers in our classroom; we also burn them on a DVD for students without internet access. Your solution to this will depend on the needs of your students, their access to technology, and the current availability of online video hosting sites. There are so many different ways to get the videos out to your students. Our suggestion is to pick one or two methods that meet the needs of your students and do them well.

How to Make Videos Your Students Will Love

So you're ready to make your own videos. You have your equipment, and you want to try flipping your classroom. We want to give you some suggestions that will make your videos better. First of all, realize that you won't make your best videos on your first try. It takes practice, trial and error, and more practice. What works for some videos will not work for others. When we first started making our own videos, they were not very good. Over time, our videos have gotten better. Give yourself some time and you, too, can make high-quality educational videos for your students. There are a few things we have learned which we now call our Cardinal Video Rules.

1. **Keep it short.** We are teaching the YouTube generation, and they want things in bite-sized pieces. If you are teaching the quadratic formula, teach just the quadratic formula. Do not teach anything else. When we first started making videos, they lasted the same length of time as our typical lectures. Most of our lectures contained multiple objectives. This is fine in a live setting, but in a video setting we have found that we need to stick to one topic per video. We try to keep our videos under 15 minutes and really shoot for under 10 minutes. Our mantra here: one topic equals one video.

2. **Animate your voice.** When you are making these videos, you are most likely using some sort of presentation software (e.g., PowerPoint, Prezi, Keynote, Smart Notebook). The only thing you have to engage your students besides your slides is your pen and your voice. Change the inflection of your voice. Make the videos exciting. We found as we got more proficient with the software, we were able to relax and be ourselves more and more in front of a computer. If you choose to make your videos live in front of students, the inflection is more natural. However, if you are talking to a computer, it is especially important to animate your voice and make it interesting. Jonathan changes his voice. He jumps into a mixture of a Russian/

German/French/Italian/Scottish/indiscernible-dialect accent on occasion. Some students find this amusing, and they never know when he might mix it up for them. Don't be discouraged if your first videos are not very good. You will get better as you make more videos. Embrace the learning process.

3. **Create the video with another teacher.** There is something powerful about watching two people having a conversation instead of watching one teacher talk at the viewer. Not often do you listen to a radio show and hear only one person talking. Think about your morning commute. When was the last time you heard only one voice? Radio stations realize that a conversation is far more engaging than a single talking head. Our students told us the same thing. Two heads (and voices) are better than one. Students learn more. Because we have both been teaching for quite some time, we know which topics students will typically struggle with, so one of us usually takes on the role of the student learning the material while the other takes on the role of an expert. Students tell us this dialogue is helpful in their comprehension of the material.

This also has been a great way to introduce other teachers to the flipped classroom. Jonathan started teaching his freshmen using the flipped-mastery model in 2009 and did it all alone. In 2010 our whole team of freshman science teachers embraced the model. For the most part, they are using Jonathan's videos. However, he is slowly making videos with different teachers. When they make them together, Jonathan runs the technology while the other teacher acts as the expert (which they really are). This has brought the other science teachers into the video production process. Some of these teachers have been reluctant to embrace the flipped model because they were simply afraid of the technology required to create the videos. Now, working with Jonathan, they realize that they can just have a conversation that is recorded for their students.

4. **Add humor.** We typically have some sort of a running joke in our videos. We usually do this for the first minute of each video. Students either love these or hate them. Because they know the joke will take up the first minute, those who like our weird sense of humor tune in, and those who don't just fast-forward. In one video series, we had a running joke in which Jonathan was trying to find out which instrument he should play. Invariably, he was poor at almost all of his instruments. Eventually he found the harmonica and played it quite well. Things like these bring interest and a certain wackiness to the videos, which helps keep the students interested.

5. **Don't waste your students' time.** Do not waste students' time. We've watched teacher-made videos where teachers talk about their favorite football team for five minutes. Students are watching this on their own time, and this sort of discussion wastes that time. Keep to your topic.

6. **Add annotations.** Think of your screen as a whiteboard with cool pictures. Use annotation equipment to add pen markups. We do not think we would ever have embraced the flipped classroom if the annotation feature had not been available. Because we primarily teach chemistry, we need some sort of a digital chalkboard to write on. Solving complex chemical problems has always involved writing. Having a way to digitally write on the screen, at least for us, allowed the flipped classroom to become a reality.

7. **Add callouts.** We incorporate a fair amount of postproduc- tion editing in which we can add callouts. A callout is a text box, a shape, or some other object that will appear for a while in the video and then disappear. Our students have found these very helpful because they bring their attention to the key elements in a video. We also use these to show steps in a problem. For example, we use the callouts to list the steps in the process. We state these steps during the recording, but also reemphasize them visually with the callouts.

8. **Zoom in and out.** In the postproduction editing, we zoom in to different portions of the screen. Often the important part of the screen is not the entire screen. Having the ability to zoom adds to student comprehension. For example, when we do a mathematical problem, we zoom in to the onscreen calculator. Or, when we are highlighting a portion of a picture on screen, we can zoom in to the portion of the picture that is most important for comprehension. This not only emphasizes a particular item, but it declutters the screen and helps the students focus.

9. **Keep it copyright friendly.** Because these videos will likely be posted online, make sure that you follow all appropriate copyright laws. We are not copyright lawyers, nor do we play them on TV. Please consult experts in this area to ensure that you do not infringe on the copyrights of others.

Class Time

Once you have set up your flipped class and made your videos, you will find yourself with extra time, a luxury you probably have never had in your career as a teacher. This leads to the inevitable question that all teachers who flip must ask, "What will I do with the additional class time?" Recently we were speaking at a conference in British Columbia, and as we presented, one young teacher asked a rather insightful question: "If I use your model, what will I do with my kids each day in class?" She realized that most of her time in class was spent standing in front of the room and talking to her students. If her "talking" was prerecorded, what would she do each day? This led to a great conversation about what kinds of activities would truly engage her students.

Despite the attention that the videos get, the greatest benefit to any flipped classroom is not the videos. It's the in-class time that every teacher must evaluate and redesign. Because our direct instruction was moved outside of the classroom, our students were able to conduct higher quality and more engaging activities.

As we have seen teachers adopt the flipped model, they use the extra time in myriad ways depending on their subject matter, location, and style of teaching. We asked some of our colleagues to share how they have changed their class time. Following are some examples.

Foreign Language Classes

In foreign language classes, teachers are recording grammar lessons and conversation starters so as to create time in class to use the language more practically. This includes having more conversation, reading literature, and writing stories, all in the target language. We visited one of these classes, a level 1 class, and observed students actively speaking Spanish. They were responding and gesturing in ways that corresponded to the teacher's instructions, which were entirely in Spanish. He would then ask students questions, and they would respond in Spanish. He reported to us how the videos had freed him up to do more of these engaging activities in his classroom.

Math Classes

Math teachers are finding the time to really help their students engage with deep analysis of mathematical concepts. Others are embracing math manipulatives and emerging technologies where students are engaged not just in learning the algorithmic computation, but in deeply wrestling with the intricacies of the math concepts. Flipped math classes are becoming laboratories of computational thinking, inquiry, and connectedness with other STEM areas (science, technology, engineering, and mathematics).

Science Classes

One concern about the flipped classroom that has been recently posed is whether flipping is compatible with an inquiry approach to teaching science. We and others have responded with a resounding *yes*. Flipping a science class creates more time and more opportunities to include inquiry learning. In science classes, teachers who flip have time for students to engage in more inquiry-based activities and to conduct more in-depth experiments. In the chemistry education community, POGIL (Process Oriented Guided Inquiry Learning; www.pogil.org), has become a powerful tool for students to create conceptual understanding without direct instruction. The flipped classroom is ideally set up for this type of learning, and we have incorporated many POGIL activities into our classroom. When a well-written POGIL activity is conducted well, the students learn all they need to learn via guided inquiry, and there is no need to teach the material with a video. In cases such as this, we use the POGIL activity as the instructional tool in lieu of a video. However, we have found that some students still use our instructional videos as a secondary resource for remediation.

Social Science/Language Arts/Humanities Classes

Social science instructors report using their extra time to discuss current events in light of the previous night's instructional video. Others are finding time to delve deeply into original document analysis. There is more time to debate, give speeches, conduct *pro se* court, and discuss what students are learning more deeply and without having to worry about a deep conversation being interrupted by a bell. There's plenty of time to write, write, write, and even more time to analyze and discuss each other's writing through peer review.

Physical Education Classes

We have been surprised to hear that some of the teachers most excited about flipped classrooms were physical education teachers. This dynamic team of teachers realized the flipped class had great potential in their courses. They told us that the most important aspect of the physical education class is for their students to be moving. Physical education teachers report that they spend too much time teaching students things like the rules of games and some of the techniques. When teachers began making videos (with a video camera) of rules, students can come to class and quickly get to moving their bodies and participating in the important physical education activities.

Project-Based Learning

Another concern is whether or not a flipped class is compatible with project-based learning. Again, we cheer *yes*. We love the idea of discovery-based learning driven by student interest. Most of us do not operate in an environment that allows for this, but educationally speaking, it is enticing and has great benefit. Picture a class driven by student-identified problems or interests. Students are exploring a real-world problem and developing solutions, and then suddenly realize that they need to know how to perform a particular mathematical function in order to execute their solution.

The teacher now faces a decision. Does she spend valuable class time teaching the entire class how to perform the appropriate math and risk boring the advanced student and losing the student who struggles? Or does she create an instructional video (or perhaps access an archived one) to give the students what they need, without sacrificing class time for direct instruction? Marrying the technological tools and asynchronous content delivery used in a flipped classroom with a student-directed approach to deciding what is learned can create an environment in which curiosity thrives. There is no need to spend time reintroducing concepts that are well established and just need to be quickly presented and learned, or to use valuable class time to deliver new content.

Student-Created Content

Flipped classrooms can give students more time to create their own content. Students today have a broad range of ways to create content to demonstrate their understanding of various topics. They can blog, create videos, create podcasts, and create many different educational products that help students build on their knowledge. We see great value in student-created content.

Chapter 5

THE
Flipped-Mastery
Classroom

Mastery learning has been around for quite some time. It was first introduced in the 1920s, but it got little attention until the 1960s, when it was popularized by Benjamin Bloom. He likened our present educational institutions to a race where only the fastest learners were rewarded. He argued that almost all students can master any content, given enough time and support. When mastery learning was implemented well, studies showed that nearly 80% of all students could learn all of the important content compared to 20% taught with the traditional model.

The basic idea of mastery learning is for students to learn a series of objectives at their own pace. Instead of all students working on the same topics at the same time, all of them work toward predetermined objectives. Mastery learning is usually done in a course with a discrete body of knowledge in which mastery of one objective is necessary for success in all subsequent objectives.

The key components of mastery learning are:

- Students work either in small groups or individually at an appropriate pace.

- The teacher formatively assesses students and gauges student understanding.

- Students demonstrate mastery of objectives on summative assessments. For students who do not master a given objective, remediation is provided.

Most of the research on mastery learning shows improvement in student achievement. Other outcomes cited are increased cooperation among students, increased student self-assurance, and students receiving a second chance at demonstrating mastery of a given objective. During the 1970s, mastery learning received a lot of attention, but it has now been largely abandoned in favor of the model seen in most brick-and-mortar schools. Most schools found it too difficult to implement the mastery system. Reasons cited for the difficulty included how often teachers must repeat themselves, how many different assessments must be written, and the difficulty of assessing so many objectives at the same time.

But we've moved on from the 1960s and 1970s. The technology explosion has made many of the difficulties of mastery learning easier to overcome. Essentially what we have done is leverage technology to make mastery possible. Our prerecorded videos have created an environment in which the burden of repetition is placed on the student. No longer is the teacher physically needed to reteach most topics. Students can simply rewatch or more fully engage with the instructional video. The teacher can then spend more quality time physically reteaching the students who most need the additional instruction.

We have also leveraged technology to solve the problem of the numerous exams necessary for a mastery model. All of our assessments are administered using computers. Each student is assessed differently from his classmates, yet the same objectives are assessed. In addition, students get a different version of the exam each time they take it. Available technology makes it much easier to have multiple assessments. The time to grade these assessments is greatly reduced because most of the questions are graded by the computer. Mountains of unsecured paper exams that must be manually graded are not necessary.

What Is a Flipped-Mastery Classroom?

A flipped-mastery classroom takes the principles of mastery learning and marries them with modern technology to make a sustainable, reproducible, and manageable environment for learning. If you were to walk into one of our classrooms, you would see much asynchronous activity. Basically, all students are working on different activities at different times. Our students are busy and engaged in their learning. You would see some students conducting experiments or other inquiry activities, some watching videos on their personal devices, some working in groups mastering objectives, some interacting with the whiteboard to engage with online simulations, some studying in small groups, and some taking assessments on either a school computer or their own personal device. You would also see some working one-on-one or in a small group with the teacher.

If you watched us throughout the class, you would observe several things: At the beginning of class we organize our students. We check to see who might need to conduct a lab, who needs to take an exam, and who needs remediation on a particular objective. You would observe us moving around the room interacting with students. We talk to every kid, in every class, every day. If a student or a group of students is ready for an experiment, we spend a few minutes discussing with them the main point of the experiment, the key safety principles, and what they should or should not be looking for. If students are ready for us to show them a science demonstration, we get a group together, demonstrate the principle, and then have a postdemonstration discussion. If students struggle on any one specific objective and need to review, you would see us working with them at the whiteboard, the SMART board, or just in a round-table discussion. If a student struggles to demonstrate mastery of any objectives on the summative assessments, we review his past attempts of the assessment with him and provide him with individualized remediation to ensure his future success. Sometimes, at this point we also provide the struggling student with an alternative form of assessment or allow the student to create his or her own way to demonstrate mastery of the objective.

You might ask how we can do so much with so many kids at the same time. Frankly, this is our struggle. We are constantly moving around the room giving attention to those who need it and making sure that all students are learning what they need when they need it. We have called this our three-ring circus of learning because there are so many different activities happening at the same time. Though as we look at a typical day, it probably should be called a ten-ring circus. Teaching in the flipped-mastery model is tiring, and our minds have to constantly switch between one topic and the next, and from one activity to another.

In order to function as an effective teacher in the flipped-mastery environment, we believe a few characteristics are necessary.

The teacher should be a content master. A teacher who is not proficient in his content area cannot operate in a flipped-mastery class. The ability to mentally move from one topic to another is necessary, and a comprehensive understanding of the interconnectedness of the content is essential.

The teacher must be able to admit when he or she does not know the answer to student questions and must be willing to research an answer *with* the student. Pride will only slow the teacher down and prove to be a detriment to student learning. The teacher should take these opportunities to demonstrate what it means to be a learner: the teacher is the lead learner in a classroom. Teachers should show students what adults do when they do not know an answer, teach them how to collaborate, and guide them through the vast ocean of information in which we swim in our interconnected world.

The teacher must be able to flow through a class period in a nonlinear fashion. All the students are at different places in their mastery and understanding of the learning objectives, and it is the role of the teacher to meet each student where she or he is. The mastery model hinges entirely on the teacher meeting the student at the point of need, not the student meeting the teacher at the prescribed place in the curriculum.

The teacher must be able to relinquish control of the learning process to the students. Control freaks need not apply.

Components of a Flipped-Mastery Classroom

Flipped mastery sounds tiring, and you might be thinking it is too much work. Let us break this down and identify the key components necessary to make flipped mastery work. There are five main components of a flipped-mastery classroom that must be in place before you start.

Establish clear learning objectives. Objectives are the desired outcomes of learning for each student. Use your state standards, national frameworks, and your best professional judgment to determine what you want your students to know and be able to do.

Determine which of these objectives are best achieved through inquiry, and which are best learned through direct instruction. Create a video for those objectives that will benefit from direct instruction. You need to have either produced your own videos, or found videos that will teach the content you want in the way you want it taught. Remember, as time goes on, more and more teachers are implementing some sort of a flipped model. Many of these teachers are making their videos available on the Internet, so you may or may not need to produce your own videos. If producing the videos seems too daunting, find someone else's.

Assure student access to videos. When you have either made or chosen other videos, you now need to make sure your students have access to them. There are a variety of ways this can be done, such as posting videos online, keeping files on school servers, and burning files to DVD. There is no easy answer to the access question, and based on our work with many schools, it seems the answer is different for each location. You will need to work with your IT department and see what will work best in your situation. We talk more about these issues in Chapter 7, which covers the nuts and bolts of the flipped-mastery model.

Incorporate engaging learning activities to be done in class. We make up a packet for each unit that contains the follow-along notes for the video, all experiments students will be doing, and all of the suggested worksheets.

Create multiple versions of each summative assessment for students to demonstrate their mastery of each learning objective in a particular unit of study. This is most efficiently and effectively done through the use of a test bank on a computer-generated testing system. We currently use the quiz module in Moodle to create and administer our exams. (More on this in Chapter 7.)

At the beginning of each unit packet we have an organizational guide that has a list of objectives, corresponding videos, reading from the textbook, learning activities, and lab activities. Our organizational guides are road maps that guide students through the unit of study and provides them with the appropriate framework and supporting activities to meet each learning objective. The following is a sample of one of these guides.

Atomic Theory Unit—Organizational Guide

Atomic-1

Objective: Be able to discuss the history of the atomic theory

Reference: Video 1; Text: 5.1; Worksheet: Atomic Theory 1

Required Activities: Cathode ray tube demo (not in packet—see teacher)

Atomic-2

Objective: Be able to determine the number of protons, neutrons, and electrons, and name of an atom

Reference: Video 2; Text: 5.2, 5.3; Worksheet: Atomic Theory 2

Atomic-3

Objective: Understand atomic mass, isotopes, and average atomic mass

Reference: Video 3; Text: 5.3; Worksheet: Atomic Theory 3

Required Activities: Vegium lab

Atomic-4

Objective: Understand the basic structure of the periodic table

Reference: Video 4; Text: 5.4; Worksheet: Atomic Theory 4

Required Activities: Annotate your periodic table

Atomic-5

Objective: Be able to explain the models of the atom

Reference: Video 5; Worksheet: Atomic Theory 5

Required Activities: Mystery tube lab (not in packet—see teacher)

Atomic-6

Objective: Explain the current quantum mechanical model of the atom as it relates to electrons

Reference: Video 6; Text: 13.2; Worksheet: Atomic Theory 6

Required Activities: Atomic Theory 6 worksheet

(Continued)

(*Continued*)

Atomic-7

Objective: Be able to write electron configurations and orbital notations for electrons for any element

Reference: Video 7; Text: 13.2; Worksheet: Atomic Theory 7

Atomic-8

Objective: Explain the wave nature of light

Reference: Video 8; Text: 13.3; Worksheet: Atomic Theory 8

Atomic-9

Objective: Explain how light reveals the "position" of electrons in atoms

Reference: Video 9; Text: 13.1; Worksheet: Atomic Theory 9

Required Activities: Flame test lab, "And Then There Was Light"

Atomic-10

Objective: Calculate the wavelength, frequency, energy, and "color" of light

Reference: Video 10; Text: 13.3; Worksheet: Atomic Theory 10

Atomic-11

Objective: Be able to compare the sizes of atoms and ions

Reference: Video 11; Text: 14.2; Worksheet: Atomic Theory 11

Atomic-12

Objective: Compare the ionization energies of different atoms

Reference: Video 12; Text: 14.2; Worksheet: Atomic Theory 12

Atomic-13

Objective: Compare the electronegativities of different atoms

Reference: Video 13; Text: 14.2; Worksheet: Atomic Theory 13

Required Activities: Periodicity graphing activity

Chapter 6

The Case for THE Flipped-Mastery Model

Now that you are familiar with the flipped-mastery model, you may be asking yourself why you should consider implementing the model. It may seem like a lot of effort to set up, and you might not be totally convinced that the model will work in your setting. Most of the reasons we cited in the chapter about why you should use the flipped model apply here as well, but the flipped-mastery model has even more benefits than the flipped model. The flipped-mastery model has completely transformed our classrooms, how we think about education, and how we interact with students. Following is a list of reasons we could never go back to a more traditional model of teaching.

The Mastery Model teaches students to take responsibility for their own learning

When we started developing the flipped-mastery model, we did not realize how it would completely change every aspect of our professional lives. Our classrooms are now laboratories of education where students take responsibility for their own learning. When we taught in a traditional model, students were there just to "sit and get." The students waited for us to tell them what to learn, how to learn it, when to learn it, and how to prove to us they had learned it. For some students this worked, but others just became disengaged and lost.

With the flipped-mastery model, the onus for learning is placed squarely on the students. In order to succeed, the students must take responsibility for their own learning. Some students are being asked for the first time to take ownership of their education. Learning is no longer an imposition on their freedom but rather a challenge to be unpacked and explored. As the teacher gives up control of the learning process, the students take the reins, and the educational process becomes their own.

At the beginning of one school year, Jonathan had one student who just wanted to "sit and get"—because it was easy and that is exactly how she was used to functioning at school. She was physically present at school, but learning usually got in the way of her social life. She just hoped to get by with minimal effort and a C. She might have been able to do this in a more traditional model, but with flipped mastery, she had to demonstrate her understanding to her teacher. During the entire first semester she butted heads with Jonathan. He kept insisting that she learn the concepts. He even caught her cheating a couple of times, but with some discussion he continued to tell her she had to demonstrate her understanding. Over time she realized that school was easier and less time consuming if she made the effort to learn the first time she encountered an assignment. She was capable, but not terribly interested. Around February, she finally decided that learning was worth her time and effort. She chose to make learning a priority. When she grasped this, she began to work ahead by watching videos before they were due, she began to fully engage in the learning process, the questions she asked her teacher about each video got deeper, and overall she became one of Jonathan's most improved students.

This story is not atypical. At first students wonder "what's up" with this unusual system. But as students begin to embrace it, they begin to develop a mature understanding of the nature of learning, knowledge, and their role in education. Most of our science students will not go on to become scientists, engineers, or doctors—but when we teach them to take responsibility for their own learning, we have taught them one of life's most valuable lessons.

I was trying to figure out how to get students from the passive mode ("you are responsible for teaching me") to the ownership mode ("I am responsible for what I learn or refuse to learn") when I came across your article in *Learning & Leading with Technology* [December/January 2008–2009]. PERFECT solution.

— JENNIFER DOUGLASS (WESTSIDE HIGH SCHOOL, MACON, GEORGIA)

The Mastery Model creates a way to easily personalize and differentiate the classroom

We frankly had no idea what would happen when we started the flipped-mastery model. We didn't read the literature. We didn't do a case study. Nor did we ask for permission from our administration. Because we believed it would be good for our students, we simply jumped in. Little did we realize that we had stumbled on an easy way to personalize and differentiate the classroom for all students.

Differentiation is a buzzword in today's educational community. When we talk to teachers around the country, most admit they are not differentiating very well because they are not physically able to meet every student's individual needs. With large classes and limited time, they feel overwhelmed. They admit that they teach to the middle of their class. If they teach their subject too fast, they leave students behind; if they go too slowly, the faster students get bored.

Flipped mastery allows the direct instruction to be asynchronous, so differentiation for each student becomes possible. The pace of the class is appropriate for each student. This personalizes the learning for each student. For example, Rachel, a future engineer, brought her teacher an assignment that she had completed to prove that she had mastered an objective. She was one of our top students who planned to eventually attend a competitive college and change the world of engineering. If there was even the slightest mistake in her work, we would send her back to find and correct the mistake. On the other hand, if Sally, who struggled greatly with chemistry, brought the same assignment to her teacher to prove her mastery of an objective, we used a different standard. We first checked for essential understanding that would ensure her success in future objectives. If those essentials were met, we would probably let a few minor errors slide.

We should point out a few qualifiers about this system. We are very careful to not let students move on without a solid grasp of essential objectives. Letting them do so would simply set them up for future failure. In addition, this short anecdote could sound as if we pigeonhole students early in the year and assess them only on our perceptions of the students. Under the flipped-mastery model, we interact with the students on such a regular basis, and we know them so well, that we constantly modify our expectations for each student as they mature as scientists and as learners. We recognize that our students are not programmable machines, but come to us with different backgrounds and needs. Our job as teachers is to be perpetually aware of those backgrounds and needs and to guide each student to the desired end in a way that is meaningful to each individual. Essentially, these differentiated, informal, formative assessments are different for every student, and our expectations change daily.

I want to teach students to pace their own learning. Students often place more importance on the letter grade they receive without understanding the material … the mastery method forces them to internalize and really understand the material to achieve the high marks they want.

— BRIAN BENNETT (AN INTERNATIONAL SCHOOL IN SEOUL, SOUTH KOREA)

The Mastery Model makes learning the center of the classroom

Walk into a classroom in which you find the teacher standing in front of the room talking to students. What is the center of this classroom? It is the teacher. If the teacher is dynamic and can clearly communicate a subject, the students are fortunate. But even then, the focus of the classroom is still on the teacher.

"The point of school is to learn." This statement, made by a student of ours, gets to the heart of flipped mastery. Our classes have become laboratories of learning where the entire focus of the classroom is on what students have or have not learned. No longer do we present material, provide a few extra learning opportunities, give a test, and then hope for the best. Instead, students come to class with the express purpose of learning. We provide them with all the tools and materials to learn, and we support them by helping them develop a plan for how and when they will learn. The rest is up to the student.

Our class is more of a conversation than simply dissemination. Students are expected to come to class and continue the process of learning or demonstrating mastery of the objectives. When learning becomes the center of the classroom, the students must work just as hard as the teacher. This means their minds are engaged, not just passively being exposed to information.

In order to help transition the focus of education from the teacher to the students, we have begun to refer to our classrooms as *learning spaces*. The word *classroom* has a lot of baggage and emphasizes the teacher as the center. It conjures up images of a teacher in front of a class with chalk in hand, disseminating knowledge to the masses. In a classroom, the teacher talks and the students listen. In a classroom, the teacher "teaches" and hopes the students learn.

When we, as educators, start calling our classrooms *learning spaces*, it will force us to change the way we think about what happens there. When we communicate this name change to our students, they will realize that the point of school is to learn, not to be taught. And as they realize the power of learning for the sake of learning, our schools will become learning spaces.

The Mastery Model gives students instant feedback and reduces teacher paperwork

The informal formative assessments mentioned in the previous section eliminate the need for a teacher to collect and mark mountains of paper. In addition, the students no longer have to wait days or weeks to get the necessary feedback on a particular assignment.

Typically, students bring completed work to their teacher and have a conversation about the key elements in an objective. During this conversation, we check for understanding and misconceptions. Instead of taking the student's work home, we are "grading" the work immediately with the student present. Students identify what they do not understand, and we discuss any misconceptions and plan the student's course of action to correct them. If mastery of the objective is demonstrated, we help the students plan the steps necessary for mastering the next objective. This is a powerful time for us to clear up misunderstandings, to challenge our bright students to take the objectives a step further, and to help students see the bigger picture. Often students learn an objective in isolation and do not see how it connects to other key topics. These one-on-one or small-group discussions get students to a deeper level of comprehension and understanding.

One teacher who has adopted the flipped-mastery model, Brett Wilie from Texas, was recently tweeting about his students' reaction to him making them prove their understanding of the content. They said, "Mr. Wilie, it was easier when we did not have to teach you. Can we go back to where we just take the test?" The students' comments about flipped mastery expose the reality that learning something deeply is a lot of work. Students under a flipped-mastery model quickly realize that the point of class is not simply to get by, but rather to thrive.

Our students take the unit assessments on classroom computers. The testing program we use grades their assessment and gives them feedback immediately. After each assessment, students notify us, and we review the exam with them. We then have a conversation about what they do and do not understand. Usually, we see a pattern of mistakes that helps us develop a proper remediation plan for the student. No longer does a student have to wait for a teacher to take tests home, grade them, pass them back, and go over the test as a class. Each student is provided the timely feedback that is essential to quickly correct misconceptions that keep them from mastering the objectives. This immediate feedback is a critical element in the flipped-mastery model because students must master the objectives before moving on to the next unit.

I have decided to make this class sound like a challenge/game. Rather than units, students will move from one "level" to the next. Rather than passing a test, they will "unlock" the next level. I think that will sound better than "Hey, look—as soon as you do these worksheets, you get to take a test! And then you get to do more worksheets!" The Desire2Learn software allows us to have a message pop up when they pass/fail a test. I would really like to have a recorded video message with different people saying, "Good job, chemistry student, you have successfully mastered this level"—or something like that. I am going to see if I can get people like Kareem Jackson—he graduated from WHS and was a 1st round NFL draft pick last year. Wouldn't that be cool? That way it would be exciting to see who was going to appear next when they passed a test! (You have to realize where we are coming from—our kids need all the motivation they can get.)

— JENNIFER DOUGLASS (WESTSIDE HIGH SCHOOL,
MACON, GEORGIA)

The Mastery Model provides opportunities for remediation

Not every student demonstrates mastery on the first attempt. What happens when a student does not learn the first time? In a traditional classroom, the class moves on with or without students who do not understand. The pace of the class is set by the teacher and is based on the material that is to be delivered on that particular day. Under this model, some students get further behind, their grade suffers, and they are penalized for being slower. We do not penalize our slower students. Instead, we give them ample opportunities to relearn and remediate.

Built into the immediate feedback is time for us to work with students and catch misunderstandings and misconceptions. As we circulate around our rooms, we are constantly giving students feedback on their learning progress. Typically this looks like one of us going up to a student or a group of students and asking to see what they are working on. We then check their progress either by examining the product they are working on or through guided questions. If we see problems in their understanding, we correct their misconceptions on the spot. This immediate feedback stops many problems from ever occurring.

Usually, there are some students in each unit who are struggling to understand some particular objectives. We identify these students and spend some time with them in small groups and hold a brief reteach/review session. According to some of the students, this attention has been some of the best learning time they have had. When students take the unit assessment, some invariably do not score satisfactorily. These students work with the teacher individually to identify the best course of remediation. What we notice is that students are not connecting all of the pieces and are failing to grasp a few key concepts. Once these misconceptions are cleared up, students are ready to move on.

The Mastery Model allows for multiple means of learning content

We recently were introduced to Universal Design for Learning (UDL), a learning theory that originated at Harvard University. The basic tenets of UDL are providing students with multiple means of representation, multiple means of expression, and multiple means of engagement.

Our primary concern is student mastery of our objectives. We realize that not all students learn best from our videos. In order to give students multiple means of representation, we provide other options for students to learn. In addition to the videos, assignments, and labs, each set of objectives references the applicable sections in the student textbook. Many students learn from our videos, others learn from textbooks, others find information about our objectives via the Internet. One size does not fit all, and we no longer require students to view the videos if they choose not to.

Allowing students choice in how to learn has empowered them. Students realize that their learning is their own responsibility. Teaching them this life lesson is more important than our science content. Students have the freedom to learn using their best learning strategies. One of the consequences of this is that students are discovering how they best learn. By giving the students the choice in how they learn something, we give them ownership of their own learning.

The assignments we give provide several ways for students to demonstrate learning. In the past we required every student to complete every problem of every assignment to our satisfaction. Now, we are at the point where we do not care how a student learns an objective—we simply want them to learn it. We provide the students with appropriate videos, worksheets, and labs that we believe will help all students master our objectives. We ask the students to essentially prove to us that they are approaching mastery of each objective.

Students who have been considered traditional failures have come to me asking me to "make" their other teachers use this method. Students who would never listen were all of a sudden listening to the videos—there is something about choosing to push the Play button that allows them to be in charge—to choose to learn. It also worked really well for students who were able to catch on at a faster rate—they loved being able to work ahead of their peers. Also, the students in special education (I did this in my collaborative classes as well) were able to work on their material with their study skills teachers—who were thrilled at being able to pick the order in which they would do their work. With each lecture, I had made several supporting tasks (labs, worksheets, mini-projects). Some students wanted to listen to all the content first, then do all the worksheets, then do the "fun stuff" (labs). Others really wanted to go in order. They each were able to select their own preference—and they enjoyed that empowerment! I rarely had students who sat and did nothing. Since they were choosing what to do they were more willing to work. The few who needed a little extra encouragement to get working were able to get it from me personally—without holding up the rest of the class.

— JENNIFER DOUGLASS (WESTSIDE HIGH SCHOOL, MACON, GEORGIA)

The Mastery Model provides multiple chances for demonstrating understanding

Another key element of UDL we have implemented is providing students with multiple methods of expression. These methods should be flexible and allow for student choice. When we started the flipped-mastery model, we insisted students get at least 75% on every unit assessment.

When we reflected on how we were assessing students, we realized one size doesn't fit all. We discussed with our students that they could demonstrate understanding of the objectives in multiple ways. We now allow students multiple ways of proving their mastery of the objectives, including

- Summative unit exams

- Verbal discussions

- Detailed PowerPoint presentations

- Short videos

- Demonstration of understanding written in prose

- Other methods developed by the students

Recently, Jonathan had a student who asked if he could just discuss what he had learned instead of writing out a detailed paragraph. Though there is certainly value in writing, his explanation was thorough and complete. He understood what was being taught, but explaining it orally was easier for him and also played into his verbal skills.

Jonathan had a student who texted him and asked if he could make a video game for his assessment. Jonathan approved his alternative assessment proposal without any idea of what the product would look like. This student, Nic, set the new bar for innovative assessments. Nic walked into class a few days after the text with his video game console, plugged it into the SMART board, and proceeded to astound us as he demonstrated the game and his understanding of the learning objectives. Jonathan was so amazed that he immediately texted Aaron. He was actually so excited, the text was unintelligible and Aaron had to go to Jonathan's classroom just to interpret the message. When Aaron arrived, he was just as dumbfounded as Jonathan was at the way the student creatively demonstrated his understanding. Aaron immediately pulled out his video camera to document this example. Shortly after, Jonathan had students clamoring to play the game, and some even asked if playing and "beating" the game levels (learning objectives) could be their assessment. This student has even recently decided to enroll in our Senior Seminar course in which he will develop more of these game-based assessments for the iPad and iPod. He hopes to leave these as a legacy for future students at WPHS and to eventually sell them on Apple's app store.

Aaron had a student who struggled with the computer based-tests. This student chose to hand-write, in prose form, everything he knew about each objective. He could clearly communicate his understanding and always provided mathematical examples that differed from any examples given in the videos or the assignments. He clearly understood the concepts but simply struggled to demonstrate his knowledge on the teacher-generated exam.

All of these students were able to clearly prove their mastery of the objectives but would not have been able to do so had we not married the UDL principles to the flipped-mastery model.

The Mastery Model changes the role of the teacher

The flipped-mastery model changes the role of the teacher. Instead of standing in front of the room spewing information and being the center of attention, we spend our time doing what is most important—helping students, leading small groups, and working with individuals who are struggling. We find ourselves walking around the room visiting with students about key learning objectives. The best analogy we can come up with is the role of a supportive coach. We are there to encourage our students along the road of learning. They need a coach who can come alongside them and guide them in the discovery of knowledge. We have more opportunities to encourage students and tell them what they are doing right and to clear up their misconceptions.

This changes the dynamics of class. Class time is a learning experience for the student, not a download and upload of knowledge. When we first started out, Jonathan in particular had a hard time giving up the direct instruction. He was a pretty good lecturer. But in time, as he saw all of his students genuinely learning, he readily gave up whole-class direct instruction.

The Mastery Model teaches students the value of learning instead of "playing school"

How often have you had students in your classroom who are good at "playing school?" They come to class more interested in getting a grade than in learning. They tend to be the first ones to ask for extra credit and tend to want rote-memory questions on exams rather than deeper, more insightful ones. Sadly, our educational system has failed these students by perpetuating an environment in which success is measured by the ability to recall information. Though they may be able to regurgitate that information for an exam, they haven't truly learned.

When these students enter our flipped-mastery classroom, they typically get frustrated. They have spent many years learning to play the game of school and have not developed the ability to really learn. Flipped mastery forces them to learn instead of memorize. We have seen tremendous growth in these students. They enter our course frustrated and leave as learners.

There are some students who have vocalized their frustrations with the process. These students most often complain because I make them retake a test or quiz when they do poorly. They really just want to get through the list of things to do, and do not care if they actually understood the material.

— MELISSA DE JONG (ROOSEVELT HIGH SCHOOL, SIOUX FALLS, SOUTH DAKOTA)

The Mastery Model is easily reproducible, scalable, and customizable

At a recent conference we received some interesting positive feedback from one of our participants. He said that flipped mastery is easily scalable. What we are doing can be reproduced and customized simply in a variety of educational settings. Practicing teachers see flipped mastery as a tool they can easily implement.

A couple of years ago, Dwight Jones, the former commissioner of education for the state of Colorado, came to visit our district. Jonathan happened to be in our central office and was brought into the conversation about the flipped-mastery model. Jones was very interested in the model and wanted to know more. We took him down to our classroom, and he had a chance to talk with a student. Afterward, Jones made an interesting comment: "And all of this happened in Woodland Park!" He caught himself, and then said he meant that it did not come out of one of the larger, richer, "premier" school districts in our state. The point is: if it can be done in our little town with minimal resources, it can be done anywhere.

To continue that point, we started this in a chemistry class—a class with dangerous chemicals and significant safety concerns! As we have shared the flipped-mastery model around the country, most people think we were crazy to develop it a chemistry class. But we saw the potential of the model, we happen to be chemistry teachers, and we thought it was best for kids. And we were right! So, if flipped mastery can be successfully implemented in a small town, with no resources, in a dangerous chemistry class, it can be implemented anywhere.

The Mastery Model increases face-to-face time with the teacher

As we began to use the flipped-mastery model, some parents expressed concern that the amount of student–teacher interaction would decrease. One parent said it well: "I have to admit I was skeptical about the [videos] at first. I had a fear that they would reduce the amount of direct contact with the students, and questions about the lectures would go unanswered. I am happy to say I was very wrong. You have come up with a way to increase the amount of teaching time for your class, and I feel my son is doing very well with it." Flipped mastery leads to much more teacher–student interaction.

Some parents were skeptical because they initially thought I wouldn't work with students in class. After meeting with some parents and explaining how it really works, most have been very receptive and excited about this method. They recognize the fact that I'm trying to respect their child's time and this method allows me to do that very easily. They also appreciate the amount of time I spend working with their children one-on-one during class time. Parents have also commented that their children who have traditionally done poorly in science classes have been doing much better with this model and that stress at home is less while doing homework because they have access to the content 24/7.

— BRIAN BENNETT (AN INTERNATIONAL SCHOOL IN SEOUL, SOUTH KOREA)

The Mastery Model ensures that all students are involved

In a flipped-mastery class, all students are in charge of their own learning. Years ago Jonathan was a trainer in the field of brain-based research and its implications in education. He often used this phrase to summarize the research, "The brain of he who is working, is growing." When you walk into a typical classroom, whose brain is usually working? In many classrooms, you see the teacher standing in front of students, probably with a PowerPoint lesson, maybe even on an interactive whiteboard, talking to the students. Sadly, it is the teacher's brain that is working the hardest, and thus growing, while the students' brains are much less active as they sit passively.

A flipped-mastery classroom looks significantly different. Students are engaged in a variety of activities: taking assessments, watching a video on a portable device, discussing a topic with their teacher, engaging in hands-on activities, and working in small learning groups. Whose brain is now working? Clearly, it is the brains of the students.

The Mastery Model makes hands-on activities more personal

Hands-on activities help students learn in a way other than direct instruction. This is particularly true in the subject of science. Students cannot just learn about science—they have to do science to learn. As students conduct experiments, they are experiencing science and constructing knowledge of scientific concepts. When done well, these hands-on activities help students question, process, and analyze what they have done.

Before flipped mastery, we would conduct these hands-on activities in a large group. The whole class would receive instructions on the experiment, and all of the students would conduct the activity simultaneously. From an organizational perspective, this is very efficient, but it is not necessarily what is best for kids. Because the flipped-mastery model is asynchronous, students conduct the experiments when they are ready to do so. The time varies from student to student. We typically work with groups of four to five students conducting an experiment. Before the experiment, we have a discussion with the group that covers the purpose of the activity and the pertinent safety concerns. Because we are discussing this in a small group, we can look the kids in the eye and see if they understand both what they will be doing and how to do it safely. Students are more engaged in these hands-on activities when they are in more intimate groups. We feel that our students are safer as a result of receiving individual-ized safety instructions.

The Mastery Model makes teacher-led demonstrations more engaging

Similar to labs, a key component in most science courses is teacher-led demonstrations. In our chemistry course we boil water by adding ice, we burn paper with steam, and we have students light us on fire. In the past, we conducted these demon-strations as part of our lecture in front of the whole class. Under the flipped model, we still did these as whole-class demonstra-tions. When we demonstrated a concept to a class of 30, only a few students in the "good seats" could see what was happening, and only a few could participate because of time constraints. In addition, only a few students (usually the bright kids who already have all the answers) participated in the discussion.

Now that our classes are asynchronous, we conduct these demon-strations when students are ready for them. This means we conduct the demonstration multiple times for a given class over the course of a few weeks in front of smaller groups of students. In smaller groups, all students can see what is happening: all of them are huddled around the interesting demonstration. In the case where our students light us on fire, it used to be that one or two students would light us on fire for any given class. Now we have all the students light us on fire. Thus, when their parents ask them what they did in school today, they can proudly say: "I lit my teacher on fire."

We find that these more personal demonstrations increase understanding. Conducting demonstrations under the flipped-mastery model allows all kids to participate in the discussion instead of waiting for the bright kid to chime in with the answer. Dividing up students into smaller demonstration groups is one of the key changes that make the flipped-mastery model so successful. Students receive a more personalized education on a daily basis.

The Mastery Model helps teachers help kids

As we visit with teachers, we find them frustrated with students who are not learning. Teachers want to do what is best for their students. Flipped mastery got us back to the reason we entered the teaching profession: to help kids. Flipped mastery is all about the students.

We began this on a shoestring budget and were able to transform our classes in a deep and fundamental way. The most remarkable aspect of our journey is realizing that we are not doing anything new! For millennia, students have been expected to come to class prepared to discuss and interact with knowledge they have already been exposed to. Unfortunately, somewhere in human history the lecture wedged its way into our instructional toolbox, and schools have been digging their way out from under its oppression ever since. We have simply adapted several very good learning principles and married them by leveraging modern technology to change the face of teaching. Mastery learning, Universal Design for Learning, project-based learning, objective/standards-based grading, and educational technology were all tapped to help create the flipped-mastery model of teaching.

Chapter 7

How to Implement
THE
Flipped-Mastery Model

So, now you are convinced. You want to implement some form of a flipped-mastery classroom. But you have questions and concerns. There are so many logistical details you need to work out. What about X? What about Y? What will this even look like in your circumstances? Although there are similarities among teachers who have flipped their classes, clearly there is no such thing as *the* flipped class, so where do you start? We have been using the flipped-mastery model since 2008, and we have made a lot of mistakes—mistakes *you* do not have to make. As we have said before, we want you to learn from our mistakes and improve on the model. One thing we have realized as more and more people adopt this model is the power of the group. We host a Ning (an online community; http://vodcasting.ning.com) where teachers who are working with some form of the flipped classroom interact. We have learned a great deal from them about how best to implement this model. Here we share answers to the most common questions about flipped mastery.

What To Do on the First Day

When we started the flipped-mastery model, we thought it would be best to ease our students into the model. We started out by getting all students to watch the same video on the same night. We essentially implemented a regular flipped model and then transitioned into a flipped-mastery model. As it turns out, that was a mistake.

In the first year of implementation, we had hoped that keeping the students together for the first unit would allow time for students to figure out any technical hurdles and for us to ease them into this model, which was so different from anything else they had encountered. We completely underestimated our students. They adapted quickly, and when we switched them from flipped to flipped mastery, we caused unnecessary confusion. As any seasoned teacher knows, the first few weeks of school are essential for establishing policies and routines. Training the students in one model and switching the procedures after three weeks is not good classroom management practice.

Now, we start the year by immediately introducing the students to the flipped-mastery model. We answer questions and spend a fair amount of time discussing how important it is for the students to take responsibility for their learning. Students watch a short video we made explaining the model. The video has clips from students in the past who give advice to students about how to be successful in this model.

Flipped mastery has become part of the culture of our science department. Our principal told us it generally takes about three years for something to become culture in a school. The first year is the hardest, the second year most of the bugs get worked out, and the third year it becomes part of the school culture. This pattern is exactly what we have experienced as we implemented the flipped-mastery model. We're now in our third year, flipped mastery is now culture, and the model is running smoothly.

Inform Parents about the Model

We inform parents by sending a letter home explaining the model. Parents need to be educated about the model because it is something new. They especially worry about our assessment method, which we will explain later. By and large, it takes constant communication with parents to help them understand both what we are doing and why we are doing it. But when we communicate to parents the advantages of the flipped-mastery model, they see how their children will benefit, and parents are generally in favor.

Early in implementation, there was some pushback from parents, but as time has gone on, they have come to accept flipped mastery as the way we do business.

Teach Students How to Watch and Interact with the Videos

An essential first step is to teach your students how to watch the videos. This is similar to teaching students how to read and use a textbook. Watching an instructional video is not like watching an entertainment movie or TV show. These educational videos need to be watched more in the way you would read a nonfiction book as opposed to a fiction book. We encourage students to eliminate distractions: they shouldn't try to watch the video with Facebook open and the iPod in the ear while simultaneously texting and making dinner. To train students, we take some time the first few days of school to watch a few videos together. We make liberal use of the Pause button. We pause the video for the students and highlight key points. At one point we give control of the Pause and Rewind features to one student. Invariably, the student in control of the Pause and Rewind buttons processes the information at a different pace than most of the class. All students want to control the video which, of course, is the point. After watching one of these videos as a class, we discuss with them how much better it would be if all of them had control of their own Pause button. Of course, they will have control for the rest of the year, but demonstrating this helps them see the value of the videos and, more importantly, their control over their own learning.

During this training period, we also teach them effective note-taking skills. There are many great ways to take notes, but we are fans of the Cornell note-taking system. We give them a template for Cornell Notes and have them use this system not only to write down key points but also to ask questions and summarize what they have learned.

Require Students to Ask Interesting Questions

When we check whether or not students have watched a video, one requirement is that they ask us interesting questions. This works especially well in our freshman Earth and Space Science course. The question must be related to the video and must be a question for which the student does not know the answer. These interactions with the students are some of the richest times we experience in our classrooms. Students ask questions either individually or in small groups. Every student must ask at least one question per video. Often during these question-and-answer times, students ask us questions for which we don't know the answer, and we work together with the students on researching the answer. The questions students ask often reveal their misconceptions and inform us of what we have not taught clearly. We then have time to clarify their misunderstandings, and we make notes of corrections to make in our videos in the future to prevent further misconceptions. These interactions are truly one of the magical moments we experience every day with our students.

Every student must ask at least one question about each video. This is especially valuable for students who do not generally interact with their teachers. In the "sit and get" model, a minority of the students ask the majority of the questions. The students asking questions are typically more outgoing and confident. The quiet, introspective students often have the same questions, but rarely voice those in the traditional model. In the flipped-mastery model all students must ask questions. We have received more and better questions in our courses than we ever did in a traditional model, and the discussions have been richer. We have found that students are curious, and in this nonthreatening format, all students can demonstrate their curiosity and learn in an individualized way.

Another thing we have noticed during the question-and-answer times is how our quiet students come out of their shells. Sadly, some of our students rarely have adults listen to them. Their parents are too busy, and their teachers are talking *to* them rather than *with* them. The only people who will listen to them are their peers. These conversational times have opened up a chance to get to know our students on a more personal level, which has paid dividends in helping troubled teens through difficult times.

Set Up Your Classroom for Flipped Mastery

We used to set up our rooms in a traditional format. The center of the room was the teacher, which usually meant all desks faced the chalkboard. As we got more technological, all desks faced the screen, which was hooked up to an LCD projector. As we began implementing our flipped-mastery model, we realized that we even needed to rethink the geography of our rooms. Now our flipped-mastery classroom is designed around learning. Instead of the focus of the room being toward the front, it is now focused toward the middle (like a kindergarten class). This shift changes the psychology of the students. They see learning as the center of the room instead of the teacher. We both have LCD projectors in our rooms, but they are rarely turned on. The focus of the room is the learning, not the teacher presentation.

We just received a grant and were able to purchase SMART boards for our rooms. The SMART boards are mounted on the side of the room instead of the front of the room. The purpose of the SMART board is for student use as an interactive tool for learning. When we first received them, one student asked if she could touch the board. She obviously had seen one in use, but it was a tool for the teacher. We have set up our SMART boards as a station where students manipulate online science simulations, collaborate on projects, and simply explore new ways of learning and understanding.

For example, in our Earth and Space Science class we use a program called Starry Night, which enables users to look at the night sky on any computer. The users can change the date and the location and have virtual telescopes. The SMART board has become a hub of activity as students flock to the board to learn about the stars. It is exciting to see students interacting with stars using technology to do what would not be possible in a regular classroom.

We teach science, and science, if done right, requires many hands-on activities. Most of these are experiments. We are often asked how we set up the experiments for a system where students could be conducting different experiments at the same time. We think the best picture is that of an elementary classroom where there are centers around the room. One center is for reading, one for writing, one for working on a computer, and so on. Our classrooms are set up in a similar fashion. We have one station for an experiment on reaction types, another set up for single replacement reactions, and another set up as an empirical formula lab. We are now using less equipment than before because only a few students are doing an experiment at a time, and safety has improved because we spend time talking to smaller groups about key safety procedures before each experiment. From a financial perspective, a flipped-mastery classroom is cheaper because only a fraction of the necessary equipment and materials are needed. You'll please your administration when you begin to operate on 20% of your former budget.

Allow Students to Manage Their Time and Workload

Jonathan's daughter was a student in his flipped-mastery class for two years. As one December approached, she became concerned about the stress of the end of a semester and her grade in her classes. Finals were in two weeks; she had a big dance recital and a church play; and all of her class assignments were due. One thing she really liked about the flipped-mastery model is that it allowed her to manage her own time. She used a good portion of her Thanksgiving break to get ahead in her dad's class. She realized her life was about to get really busy, so she chose to work ahead. She realized she could take her final once she mastered all of the semester objectives. So, she planned her time so the rest of her upcoming schedule was not quite as crazy. She took and passed her final exam early and was able to focus on her other classes. She even used her dad's class time as an opportunity to prepare for her other class finals.

She is not alone. One thing we're noticing about our students is they are learning to manage their own time. They know which objectives need to be mastered by a particular time. They can pace their schedules and learn to make good choices about priorities and time management.

Jonathan's daughter was a conscientious student who wanted to excel. You are probably asking, What about students who don't take as much initiative? We have found our flipped-mastery classes to be great growing experiences for our students. Those who come in with few time-management skills learn to manage their time. We give students freedom to make both good and bad choices. As the year progresses, students begin to make better and better choices. We see this with our struggling student population as well as our honors students. Though this is not the magic bullet for developing all students' time management skills, it certainly has led to growth for most of our students.

Encourage Kids to Help Kids

We describe our classes as hubs of learning. The focus of the classroom is no longer on the teacher, but rather on the learning. Subsequently, students realize that learning is the goal and turn to each other for help. They automatically organize themselves into learning groups. It is very common for us to walk by a group, ask about what they are learning, and see students helping others.

We also place students into strategic groups. We find students who are struggling with the same content and assemble a spontaneous group. This dynamic keeps the class from becoming a place in which 30 students are conducting independent study. The small groups maintain the classroom dynamic by encouraging interaction, collaboration, and exploration.

All of this excites us. Our students realize they are better when they work as a team rather than when they work alone. This gets at the heart of 21st-century learning: students working together to accomplish the same goals. We realize they will soon enter the world of work, and people rarely work in isolation. The students will become part of teams solving problems, and the flipped-mastery model is set up to encourage this kind of interaction.

I have noticed an increase in cooperative work in my room … students have naturally formed consistent study groups to work with during each class. This has also been a negative because some of the groups are not productive when working together.

— BRIAN BENNETT (AN INTERNATIONAL SCHOOL IN SEOUL, SOUTH KOREA)

Build an Appropriate Assessment System

Certainly one of the biggest challenges in our model has been our struggle to build an appropriate assessment system that objectively measures student understanding in a way that is meaningful for the students and the teacher. How do we know if our students have mastered the course objectives? What do we do when students do not get it? These questions invariably present a challenge to those interested in adopting the flipped-mastery model. But fear not—we have learned the hard way, so you do not have to.

The logistics of managing multiple versions of one assessment is possibly what derailed the mastery movement in the 1980s. Creating multiple versions of quality assessments, managing the paper, and keeping track of test security is just too overwhelming for one teacher with 30 students in a room. We believe that leveraging modern technology to provide valuable feedback to our students and to aid us in implementing the flipped-mastery model is what makes mastery possible.

Formative Assessments

Both of us have taught chemistry for many years, and over that time we have developed enough background in our subject to quickly tell whether a student understands key points. As we move around the room and interact with students, we spot-check their understanding. While students are in the process of learning, we discover and correct misconceptions. We recognize that as students develop concepts, they require different levels of support depending on their individual cognitive development as well as the cognitive load of a particular objective. At times, we provide a student with very structured assistance, but in other situations, we allow students to struggle. We realize that learning is not a matter of spoon-feeding the content to the students. It is appropriate for the teacher to allow a student to wrestle with a difficult concept so that the student learns it deeply. So, some students we leave alone because we know their learning will be much deeper than if we hold their hand throughout, and we proceed to provide support to students who need it.

The burden of proof in the formative process is placed on the student. We provide students with learning objectives and the resources necessary to meet those objectives, but the students are required to provide evidence to the teacher that the objective is being learned. For students who can't prove that they are making progress toward the objective, we quickly assess their understanding and create a customized remediation plan on the spot so students can go back and learn what they have not yet mastered. The types of remediation and reteaching vary from student to student. We may ask students to rewatch a video or, in some cases, to watch it for the first time. We give them textbook resources to consult and web pages to visit, or we may simply sit down with them and work through the concepts that weren't understood. We used to refer to the formative assessment process as "checking the oil," but education speaker and design thinking advocate Ewan McIntosh (www.notosh.com/about/ewanmcintosh/) corrected us and equated formative assessment to a GPS. When a driver using a GPS begins to go astray, the GPS "recalculates" the route to help the driver get back on track. The driver can continue to ignore the GPS and will either eventually listen to the GPS and get back on track, or drive into a lake. In the classroom, the teacher can be the voice of the GPS redirecting students when they go astray in their understanding. Students can accept the advice and redirection of the teacher, or they can drive themselves into the cognitive lake of misconception.

It is the responsibility of the teacher to constantly evaluate each student's path and provide immediate feedback that will keep the student traveling safely through the highways of learning. Ultimately, the key questions are always, Did you learn it? And if you did, can you provide evidence that you have? However, part of good teaching is knowing where the student is along the journey, not just checking to see if they arrived safely.

Asking the Right Formative Assessment Questions

As we interact with our students, we are constantly having a dialogue with them. We are making sure they understand the learning objectives. We are prodding them and pushing them to learn as deeply as they can. A key component of this is our questioning strategy.

Some time ago we sat down with the dean of the school of education at a private university. She was most curious about this aspect of the flipped-mastery process. She asked us how we would train new teachers in our methodology. She pointed out that we were veteran teachers who intuitively know which questions to ask. How do we communicate this to prospective teachers?

This is a tricky question to answer, because intuition is not easily transferable. We deliberately take time early each school year to discover and understand how each student thinks and learns. We do not do this with any formal battery of assessments; we simply talk to our students and get to know them. Our method is highly subjective, but it works. So, our advice to other teachers interested in adopting the flipped-mastery model is to talk to your students, get to know them as the amazing people they are, learn how they think, and help them learn how to learn.

The teacher must ask the right question for each student. Because we know our students well, and because we know to what extent they understand each learning objective, we vary our questions based on student understanding. Each student is at a different level of comprehension, and our main goal is growth.

One advantage of flipped mastery is that the teacher gets a lot of practice asking questions. Instead of asking the question one time during a lecture, you get to ask students as you interact with each of them. Practicing the flipped-mastery model will help prospective teachers by giving them ample opportunities to tailor specific questions to students and meet their individual learning needs.

Summative Assessments

Our formative assessments are essential in checking student understanding, and they are fundamental in the formation of student content knowledge. However, we believe that students also need high-stakes assessments in which they demonstrate their mastery of learning objectives. Thus, we have developed summative assessments for which students must demonstrate a minimum level of proficiency.

Various models of assessment exist for the educator. Exams can be scored out of total points, objectives can be assessed individually on a 0–4 scale, or a test can represent a straight percentage. We live in an A–F world where percentages determine a student's letter grade. Although we do not entirely believe in assessing students using a percentage, we nonetheless have to operate under a less-than-ideal framework. In order to function in the A–F environment that parents, students, and administrators are comfortable with, we have decided that students need to score a minimum of 75% on every summative assessment in order to prove mastery. This number is not arbitrary. We look at the essential learning objectives and create the test in such a way that a student who has mastered the key objectives will score a 75%. The other 25% of the assessment can be earned by mastering the "nice to know" objectives that are also a part of our curriculum, but may not be essential for success in subsequent lessons. A student who does not score 75% or higher must retake the assessment. If a student struggles with a specific topic, we provide remediation to him or her, giving the support the student needs to master each summative assessment. We also allow a student to retake an assessment if a 75% is attained, but the student desires a higher score. We leave this up to students because we are also trying to teach them to take responsibility for their own learning.

We have a number of laboratory assessments students must complete. In these assessments, students are given a problem to solve. They then use available equipment, chemicals, and materials to work out the solution to the problem. These authentic assessments are also a key part of our program. Students also need to score a minimum of 75% to move on with these. One of the benefits of the flipped-mastery model for the students is that they are not allowed to turn in junk. If they submit unacceptable reports, we simply hand them back and make them fix their work. Students who are just trying to "get by" quickly discover that they are better off turning in quality work the first time instead of poor work they will have to redo.

Also note that although the process just described is the one we employ, it is not the only way to use summative assessment in a flipped-mastery setting. Many teachers and schools who have flipped administer summative assessments in a more traditional manner. The test is given to all students on a particular day, and whatever score is attained is permanent. There is no single way to flip, no single way to assess, and no single way to give students feedback. As always, do what is best for your students and operate within the parameters of your particular educational setting.

Test Integrity

When we first started the flipped-mastery program, we used paper tests. Granted, we had multiple versions, but students took the exams at different times, often in less supervised environments. Unfortunately, some of our students made poor choices and found ways to cheat on the exams. Some took pictures of the test with cell phones and shared those with their friends. Quickly, some of our exams got out into the wild among the student population.

Implementing computer testing helped with security, but even then we found students who would copy and paste whole exams, send the copy to their home account, and distribute it to their friends. Needless to say, we were frustrated and discouraged. Because of the lack of computers in our classroom, we sometimes sent students to the school library to take exams. Sadly, we discovered students taking their exams in a group, or with notes or other unallowable materials.

We are not naïve—we realize that some students will always try to get around the rules and will make poor choices. Our role as good teachers is to limit the opportunity of students to cheat. With a few subtle adjustments, our present solution has solved most of our security issues. We now allow exams to happen only in class. We have set up several computers (six to seven) in our rooms. Each test is password protected, and we are the only ones who know the password. When a student is ready for an exam, the student logs on to his or her own account, and then the teacher types in the password. This gives us a chance to chat with individual students before the exam and check to see that they have allowable references (for example, a periodic table and calculator). Usually, we give them an encouraging comment. Though this is not a perfect system, most of the integrity issues have been solved.

Those who want to take the integrity issues one step further can do what Aaron began in 2011: administer open-Internet tests. He began this experiment to answer two questions: (1) what questions are so easy to find answers to on the Internet that they do not need to be taught in class, and (2) given that so much information is at the fingertips of our students, how will the exams need to be written differently in order to effectively evaluate what the students know and can do with a certain subject? Asking these two questions is transforming his tests from primarily data-recall and mathematical computation to problem solving, data analysis, and mathematical understanding. In addition, test integrity is less of an issue because the answers cannot be easily shared as a result of the open-ended nature of the questions.

Logistics of Summative Assessments

When mastery learning was being encouraged in the 1980s, the logistics of assessment may have been one of the main challenges that derailed widespread adoption. How does a teacher manage so many versions of a test? If we keep giving students the same exam over and over, eventually they memorize the test, but still don't understand the content. When we began the flipped-mastery model, we simply wrote a few pen-and-paper versions of each exam. Unfortunately, students did just what we feared: they memorized the exams. Although they passed the test, they had not truly learned.

One thing we did to help us with the logistics of having to grade so many exams that were being taken at different times was to turn to computer-generated exams. Our school adopted a free, open-source course management program called Moodle, and we began to see if this would work for us. It showed great promise because it immediately graded the exams, which took a huge burden off of us. However, we still had the problem of too few versions of the exam that were too similar.

One day, Jonathan was reading a help forum online about Moodle. It explained a way to create a unique version of each test for every student. Each student also gets a different version for each attempt. When we write our questions, we create multiple questions that assess each objective. Then, when we build our exam, we have the computer randomly choose one or more questions from each objective. Doing so creates tens of thousands of versions of each test, solving the logistical problem of multiple versions. This truly made mastery manageable.

Be warned, though: this represents an enormous amount of work. Instead of writing one or two questions for each objective, we now write 10 to 20. This is a huge commitment for us. We are also continuing to refine this process and add more questions, change the way questions are worded, and make sure the essential objectives are accurately and adequately assessed. We see this as a multiple-year project that ultimately is never done.

If you are looking for course-management software in addition to Moodle, there are many other great programs out there, including Blackboard and WebCT.

Working within the A–F Grading Culture

We imagine many of you work in an environment similar to ours. In our school, students still receive credit for a course completed. As teachers, we still must give all students a grade: "A" for excellent, "B" for above average, "C" for average, "D" for below average, and "F" for failing. We had to figure out a way to make a mastery system work in this context. At first this was a real struggle. We see our class in more of an objective-based or standards-based grading framework, but our school is not set up to operate under such a model. In addition to working a mastery model within the confines of an A–F system, we also are required to input our grades into the online grade book that our district has adopted. This grade book is visible to parents who are accustomed to seeing all grades listed as percentages or points and calculated as a letter grade. To address these challenges, we have gone through several iterations and much reworking of our grading system.

For what it is worth, we have come up with a hybrid system that is part objective-based grading and part traditional A–F grading that may or may not work in your setting. In our system, we make summative assessments worth 50% of a student's grade. Students must score at least 75% on each summative assessment before a grade can be entered into the grade book. The other 50%

of the grade is for timely progression toward mastery of individual formative assessments.

A flipped class is ideally suited to a standards-based grading (SBG) system. Many who flip do not use SBG, and many who do not use SBG do not flip; however, the two work well together. The Adams-50 school system in Westminster, Colorado, has adopted a district-wide standards-based grading system. In any given class, students can be at different grade levels, and any given student can be at different grade levels in each of his or her classes. The district instructional coaches recently discovered how well their grading system works with asynchronous video instruction, and many of their teachers are now creating videos to meet the instructional needs of their students.

Every grading environment in schools across the world is different, and we all have to operate within the parameters in which we teach. Introducing a flipped class is often a radical enough change that some may be hesitant to alter an existing grading system. This component of a flipped-mastery class will vary as much from school to school as the distribution of videos does.

Chapter 8

Answering YOUR
Questions (FAQs)

By now, we hope you have seen the benefit of the flipped classroom, and have begun thinking about how to implement it in your setting. We have been compiling answers to questions we have received over the past few years and we hope your burning inquiries are addressed here. We hope you can learn from our mistakes.

Clearly there is more than one way to implement a flipped classroom, so what do all flipped classrooms have in common?

Believe it or not, not all flipped classrooms use videos as an instructional tool. A flipped classroom does not center around videos, but most teachers who flip use videos as a means of delivering direct instruction. The one unifying characteristic of all flipped classrooms is the desire to redirect the attention in a classroom away from the teacher and onto the learners and the learning. In order to do this, most flipped classroom teachers ask one question: Which activities that do not require my physical presence can be shifted out of the class in order to give more class time to activities that are enhanced by my presence? Most (but not all) teachers who flip have answered this question with "lectures" or "direct instruction." Granted, you do not have to flip your class to turn the attention away from the teacher, and there are many valuable educational models and tools that help a teacher do so. A flipped classroom is one of those tools, but it is not the only tool available to do so.

What do you do with kids who don't have access to a computer at home?

Our school is located in a relatively rural area of Colorado. Many of our students live in places where there is no reliable Internet access. In fact, it was 2008 before Aaron was finally able to get high-speed Internet access at his home. When we started flipping, and at the time were requiring that *all* students watch our videos, we realized that we needed to make sure *all* kids had access to them.

We posted our videos in many different places so students would have choices of where to access them. For those students with high-speed access, we posted them online at a couple of video sharing sites. We put videos on our school district server, and students with computers at home who had either inadequate or no Internet access loaded the videos on flash drives and viewed them at home. Many students also brought their iPods, cell phones (yes, the videos can be placed on cellular phones), and other portable media players, and we loaded the videos onto their personal devices. For those students who didn't have access to computers, we created and burned DVDs that students could put into a DVD player and watch on their TV. Aaron was even able to fix up some donated computers and put them in the hands of students with no computer at home.

One increasingly common concern about the flipped class is that it could contribute to an even greater "digital divide" between the haves and the have-nots. So far, we have not had any students claim that they did not have access to either a personal or public computer, a portable device, or a DVD player. We are open to criticism on this point, but we believe that lack of equitable access is not an insurmountable obstacle and can be overcome with a little creativity and resourcefulness. Those interested in educational technology must do everything in their power to bridge the digital divide. Our suggestion: write grants. Not one, not five, but as many as you can humanly crank out. This is exactly how we overcame the problem of inadequate technology in our classrooms. We wrote and received numerous grants to outfit our classes with interactive whiteboards, netbooks, and wireless infrastructure and found it to be an effective way to pursue bridging the digital divide.

How do I know if my students watched the video?

If students are required to watch a video as their homework, how can you know if they have done so? When we were requiring students to view our videos, we started by trying to figure out some high-tech way to check whether they had viewed it. We considered using a website where students would log in to view the video, and we would check the viewing log for participation. But then Jonathan had an idea that was extremely low tech and simple: "Why don't we just check their notes?" And to this day, that is exactly what we continue to do. Students take notes from the videos, and we simply check that notes have been taken in some form. We have expanded the format slightly, letting students take paper notes, but also allowing them to post comments on a blog or to email their teacher. One element that began in Jonathan's earth science/astronomy class has completely changed the way we interact with our students. We ask all of these students to both show their notes and individually ask their teacher an interesting question that they thought of while viewing the video. This individual question-and-answer time is very powerful because it requires all students to interact with their teacher on an almost daily basis. In this model, it isn't just the bright, curious students who ask questions—it's also the shy or disengaged students who would never dare to raise their hands in a typical classroom.

Once again, be reminded that there are many ways to ascertain whether or not students have viewed a video. Ramsey Musallam, a teacher in San Francisco, embeds his videos and a Google Form onto a web page. After viewing a video, or even while viewing a video, his students comment and respond to prompts in the embedded form and submit their form electronically. Brian Bennett has his students write in their blogs every day and reflect on their learning. Be innovative and make this work in your setting, or even consider making the videos optional and use a different method to formatively assess your students' understanding.

What about kids who don't watch the videos?

Because the vast majority of the direct instruction is delivered through videos, students who do not watch them are not prepared for class. In fact, nonviewing students will totally miss important content. It is as if they had skipped the class in a traditional classroom. Our solution to this problem was relatively simple. In each of our classrooms we have two computers in the back of the room. Students who do not watch the videos at home are allowed to watch them in class. Nonviewing students who have to use class time to watch the video miss out on the tutorial time, where the teacher walks around and helps students. Because all assignments are now done in class, these students have to complete their assignments at home as in a traditional model. Students quickly realize that it is to their benefit to have the teacher as a resource when working on their assignments, and most take the time to view the videos at home so they can take advantage of the time with the teacher. We find this to be a good motivator for the vast majority of our students.

How long are the videos?

When we first started making the videos, we made each one the length of our typical lecture. The videos usually included several different topics. The feedback from our students was that they preferred shorter videos including only one objective per video. We try to restrict most of our videos to between 10 and 15 minutes, and we wish they were 5 minutes. We have found that chunking the videos into smaller segments helps the students learn better.

Doesn't flipping increase homework time, especially if students watch videos for multiple classes?

At least in our case, the amount of time students spend viewing videos is approximately the same amount of time they used to spend doing homework. And in many cases this is reduced because in the traditional model, students who struggled with the content spent a much greater amount of time on the assignments they didn't understand. Our students who have more than one class with a video assignment don't report a greater amount of homework than before.

Another common concern that comes up regarding homework has to do with whether or not homework should even be given. We are not going to discuss the philosophical and practical matters of whether homework has a place in education, but we do have some insight if you would like to flip your class in a setting with a no-homework culture or policy. A teacher interested in flipping in a setting such as this would have to design her class so that all the work (viewing videos, class work, assessment) could be done in class during school. This would most likely look like an asynchronous mastery class. Interestingly, some of our more efficient students have realized that they work quickly enough to complete all their work in our classes. These students don't do anything, including watching videos, outside of class.

Remember, a flipped class does not have to have videos, nor do the videos have to be viewed at home. The goal of flipping a classroom is to remove attention from the teacher and place it on the learner. If videos are to be used, and if they are to be viewed in class, then adequate and equable access to appropriate technology must be in place before embarking on this endeavor. This should not dissuade the potential "flipper," but it must be addressed before moving in this direction. It would be unethical to create an educational environment in which some students could participate and others could not. But conscientiously dealing with equity issues before embarking on a flipped class would allow any teacher to adopt the model in any circumstance. As educators we must never dismiss a teaching tool simply because the potential for inequity exists. Just because a flipped classroom would not be appropriate in one setting does not mean it should not be adopted in another setting. We should think creatively, solve the problem at hand, and pursue what is best for our students. Inequity exists only because we let it exist. Create an equitable learning environment and proceed; if you cannot create an equitable environment, then do not flip.

How did you get your administration to buy in?

When we started flipping our classrooms, we just jumped in. We didn't get any preapproval from our administration—we just started. We have a great school with supportive administrators, and we have always felt free to do what is best for kids. Shortly after we started flipping, our assistant superintendant came down to our classrooms and wanted to see what was happening. After seeing so many students engaged in learning, she invited us to share our model with our school board. Our message was well received by the board, and they fully supported the changes we were making because they saw how valuable it was for our students. In fact, when we told them about our challenges, they responded by updating our inadequate teacher computers.

You may wonder what challenges you might face when presenting the model to your administrators. We simply do not know. We were lucky. Others we know who have flipped have had to go through a lengthy process of providing rationale and research that the model works. One successful story that we know of began with a teacher committing to flipping one instructional unit from her curriculum. She invited her principal to see the students learning, and after seeing how engaged the students were, the principal quickly gave her the green light to proceed.

Giving support to this type of initiative is simple because of the concept behind it. Decisions about the best type of education to be given should be made by those closest to the outcomes. The only difficult part of the process is tackling the unforeseen circumstances that occur. Obstacles can always be worked so the system works.

— DEL GARRICK (PRINCIPAL, WOODLAND PARK HIGH SCHOOL, WOODLAND PARK, COLORADO)

How did you get parents to buy in?

We have a very supportive parent community. When we started flipping the classroom, the biggest concern was over access to the videos. Because we solved that problem with DVDs, most parents were curious about the new approach. Once we explained the reason for the flip, most parents understood and were supportive. During back-to-school night, and in a letter to the parents, we explain what the flip is and why we flipped. What we have found is that consistent, clear communication goes a long way when introducing something new. The flipped classroom is very different from what our parents have experienced, but the vast majority of them are appreciative.

Jonathan had one parent who initially expressed concern about the model. She thought that we were conducting an online class, and that her daughter would not be interacting with her teacher on a regular basis. Once she fully understood the model, she emailed Jonathan and thanked him for actually *increasing* the interaction with her daughter. She noted that under the flipped classroom her daughter was able to access her teacher more easily than under a lecture model.

What do you do with students who do not buy in?

We wish we had a silver bullet to solve all the problems of education. However, we do not. What we can offer to address this question is this: before we introduced the flipped classroom we had roughly a 10% failure rate, with the flipped classroom we had roughly a 10% failure rate, under the flipped-mastery model we have roughly a 10% failure rate. Unfortunately we do not have an answer to this and we have not been able to solve this issue. What we can say is this: because we know our students better as a result of spending more time with each kid individually, we have noticed that each of our failing students has a story. Most of them have a difficult life situation, and school is simply not their priority. Knowing them better allows us to provide them the support they need.

One student in particular expressed great frustration with the flipped-mastery model and angrily cursed at Jonathan. After speaking with the student on a deeper level, we and his counselor were able to uncover some underlying problems in his life. Although he still failed the class, he was able to get the help he needed from the counselors. The flipped-mastery model is not directly responsible for this student receiving the help he needed, but it did let us know him much better than we would have in a traditional classroom and point him in a more positive direction.

Does it work? Do students learn better with the flipped model?

When we started flipping the classroom, we had no idea whether it was sound educational practice—we just did it. (That was probably not the wisest way to go about it, but it is what it is.) So, do students learn better in a flipped classroom, and how do we know?

At the time of publication of this book, we know of some action research being conducted on the flipped classroom, but very little has yet been completed and published. We hope to see more in the near future and plan to interact with the research as it emerges. In the meantime, here are our anecdotal observations.

When we both started teaching chemistry at Woodland Park High School, we taught using the traditional lecture method. In order to have a consistent program throughout our school, we decided to give the same exams to all chemistry students regardless of teacher. This set of class test scores from 2006–07 students gave us a basis for comparison. When we flipped the classroom the next school year, we decided to give exactly the same tests and see what happened.

Before we share the results, we need to explain a couple of things. When we started teaching at WPHS, we took over from a long-time teacher who had retired. This teacher accepted only the best and brightest students into her chemistry classroom. Her prerequisites were very stringent for students entering into chemistry. So the first year we taught, we had an exceptional group of students who had met these prerequisites and had extremely high incoming scores on the Colorado State Exam (see Table 8.1). We looked at each other and asked ourselves if we had ever seen such amazing kids.

TABLE 8.1 Incoming Scores on Colorado State Exam: Scores for 2006–07 Students

	Reading	Writing	Math	Science
Average score	714	635	646	534

We both strongly believed that the previous teacher's chemistry prerequisite (current enrollment in Algebra II) was too stringent. We decided to lower the prerequisite math requirement (current enrollment in Geometry) in order to encourage more students to challenge themselves and take chemistry. The following year enrollment expanded when we lowered the math prerequisite, going from an enrollment of 105 students to 182 students. As might be expected, the incoming scores on the Colorado State Exam for this expanded group were lower (see Table 8.2).

TABLE 8.2 Incoming Scores on Colorado State Exam: Scores for 2007–08 Students

	Reading	Writing	Math	Science
Average score	699	607	619	519

During the 2007–08 school year, we taught using the flipped classroom model, but we used the same exams to assess our students. By the end of the school year, we had collected a second set of class test scores that could be directly compared to the first set. It was time to find out how the two sets of students did on the same exams. We might have expected that, based on their lower Colorado State Exam score averages, the 2007–08 students would also score lower on their class tests. But as it turns out, our group of students who were taught using the flipped classroom scored almost the same average scores on the same tests as the previous year's students who learned under the traditional lecture model (see Table 8.3).

TABLE 8.3 Comparison of Class Test Scores

	2006–07 Students Average Score	2007–08 Students Average Score
Unit 1 Exam	Different exam given	
Unit 2 Exam	78.7%	78.7%
Unit 3 Exam	84.5%	86.8%
Unit 4 Exam	81.6%	80.7%
Unit 5 Exam	Different exam given	
Semester 1 Final	67.9%	66.2%
Unit 6 Exam	75.1%	74.1%
Unit 7 Exam	89.0%	81.2%
Final Exam	73.9%	71.7%

One exam that concerned us was Unit 7, where the score varied the most from one year to the next. We racked our brains and wondered why our students did not perform as well. When we looked at the calendar for the 2007–08 year, we realized that because of snowstorms, our students in the 2007–08 group (the flipped group) had approximately two weeks to learn the content, whereas the 2006–07 group had almost four weeks for the same content. All other exams for the flipped group were either higher or statistically insignificantly lower.

This is obviously not a robust scientific study, but it seems to indicate that through the flipped class model we were able to help students with lower math skills perform at a similar level as a group with higher math skills in a mathematically heavy science class.

Our verdict—the flipped classroom worked!

Most students have been very receptive and have excelled with this model. Others have required a lot more of a push from me to stay on top of their work. I have not seen a significant increase in low achievement (C– or below) from traditional teaching, but I have seen an increase in high achievement, especially from students who describe themselves as weak in math and science.

— BRIAN BENNETT (AN INTERNATIONAL SCHOOL IN SEOUL, SOUTH KOREA)

Who makes the videos?

When we first started, we made all of the videos individually. Aaron would make Unit 1 of chemistry while Jonathan would make Unit 1 of AP chemistry. We would then flip which teacher did which class. As time went on and we made version 2 of our videos (our first ones were not very good), we began to create them together. Making the videos together improved their quality significantly. The videos are now more of a conversation about science instead of the dissemination of scientific knowledge. As our videos began to receive some notoriety, we heard from teachers around the country that they were using our videos as supplements in their classrooms or, in some cases, as the primary means of instruction in their classes. It is OK to use someone else's videos! You do not have to make these on your own. There is certainly value in a student hearing her teacher's voice, reading her teacher's handwriting, and seeing her teacher's face on the instructional video. But to get started, you might consider using some that are already made by other teachers. Then gradually make your own and phase the others out.

How do you find time to make the videos?

Because we had committed that first year to making *all* of our lectures ahead of time, we somehow fit it all in. Jonathan is a morning person, and you would often find him at school at 6:00 a.m. making chemistry videos. Aaron, being the night owl, would be found in his laundry room making videos after he put his kids to bed. Somehow we made it work. When we committed to doing them together, we would often come in before school or stay late and get them done. This certainly was a heavy time commitment. But now that we have those videos done, only a few need to be tweaked every year. In fact, all our "extra time" has allowed us the opportunity to finally write this book! In all likelihood, we would be sitting here after school today, at the same computer we are using to write this book, but we would be producing one of our videos.

Chapter 9

Conclusion

Although we know that the lecture is not the best means of communicating information to students, sometimes direct instruction has a place. However, that place is not in the classroom, and not in a whole-class setting. We have also learned that delivering instruction with a video can be very effective for some topics, but not as effective for others. Some concepts must be discovered independently by a student, others are best taught directly, and others under a Socratic dialogue. Our videos are not the end-all of education, but they have allowed us to better explore models of education that are best for our students. We encourage you to explore and hybridize what you have learned from us, adapting it to what you already know to be good teaching practice.

I wouldn't ever fully switch back to a traditional classroom. Right now, I am actually using a hybrid method. Mondays are short periods (45 minutes) each week and then the rest of the week alternates on a block schedule. On Mondays, I usually live-teach major topics for those students who need face-to-face interaction in the room. It also allows me to address major issues that are coming up in the content with many of the students.

— BRIAN BENNETT (AN INTERNATIONAL SCHOOL IN SEOUL, SOUTH KOREA)

Not all concepts are best taught using the same techniques; as such, some things are still taught traditionally, some concepts are taught through student discovery, and some through the flipped classroom. We look at the exit skills we want and plan thinking of the best methods to teach the students.

— PHILIP KURBIS (MUNICH INTERNATIONAL SCHOOL)

Developing what has grown to be known as the flipped classroom has been quite a journey for both of us. We have been humbled by observing the explosion of something that started in a couple of classrooms in rural Colorado and in other scattered places, but now has spread around the world. We were simply a couple of teachers who wanted to do what was best for students and jumped in. We didn't realize the implications of what we stumbled on. Now, however, we realize that the flipped and flipped-mastery models have the potential to make a positive impact on education.

We also want to acknowledge all the educators and students who have grown with us through this process and have influenced our thinking about the flipped classroom. This book shares our story from our perspective, and we know that many other amazing educators have been using these same tools, skills, and resources for years. We wish to recognize Lage, Platt, and Treglia for their publication of "Inverting the Classroom: A Gateway to Creating an Inclusive Learning Environment" in the winter 2000 *Journal of Economic Education*. We can only hope that the wisdom and experience of others continues to shape the flipped classroom.

So much of what we practice on a daily basis was inspired by other teachers using similar instructional tools and adapted to meet our needs. We do not claim to have invented some new pedagogy, and we have not tried to brand an innovation. We simply saw a need and met it with an available technological tool—and have been so excited with the results that we felt compelled to tell the world.

If you are considering flipping your classroom, we want you to be sure you are doing it for the right reasons. As we stated earlier in this book: control freaks need not apply. One of the hardest things we had to do when switching to the flipped and ultimately the flipped-mastery model was to give control of the learning over to the students. For many educators, this is very difficult. But when learning is in the hands of the students and not in the hands of the teacher, real learning occurs. Strong constructivists and die-hard project-based learning advocates will say that we have not gone far enough in handing over the learning to our students. They may be right. However, flipping the classroom is an easy step than any teacher can take to move away from in-class direct instruction to more student-directed and inquiry-based learning.

As we share our story around the country, we hear over and over from teachers, administrators, parents, and most importantly students how much they want the flipped model implemented. Teachers who went into education to help kids see these models as a way to achieve their ultimate goal of teaching. Administrators like the fact that flipping the classroom is scalable, reproducible, and customizable and doesn't require a great deal of money. Parents love the models because they see this as a way for their children to learn deeply instead of just being exposed to information. And last, and most important, students appreciate the models for so many reasons: (1) it speaks their language, (2) it teaches them to take responsibility for their own learning, and (3) it is flexible and allows them to work at the pace that works best for them.

We both believe that good teaching happens in the context of healthy student–teacher relationships. Students need to see adults as mentors and guides instead of experts from on high. Teachers need to see students not as helpless kids who need to be spoon-fed their education, but rather as unique individuals who require a unique education. The flipped and flipped-mastery models have allowed us to empower students to want to learn more content more deeply in an interactive, relationship-rich environment that helps them succeed.

Now we charge you, our reader, with the challenge to go out and do whatever it takes to think differently about education. Though you may not adopt our models fully, we encourage you to ask one question: "What is best for kids?" Then go and do it.